WITH THE SKIN

WITH THE SKIN

Poems of Aleksander Wat

TRANSLATED AND EDITED BY
CZESLAW MILOSZ AND LEONARD NATHAN

The Ecco Press
New York

Copyright © 1989 by Paulina Wat
Translation © 1989 by Czeslaw Milosz and Leonard Nathan
Introduction © 1989 by Czeslaw Milosz
All rights reserved

Published in 1989 by
The Ecco Press
26 West 17th Street
New York, NY 10011
Published simultaneously in Canada by
Penguin Books Canada Ltd., Ontario
Printed in the United States of America
FIRST EDITION

*The editors gratefully acknowledge the assistance of
David Brodsky and Stephen Grad in the translation of
"Songs of a Wanderer," and Richard Lourie in the translation
of "Dreams from the Shore of the Mediterranean."*

Library of Congress Cataloging-in-Publication Data

Wat, Aleksander.
  [Poems. English. Selections]
  With the skin / Aleksander Wat
  translated and edited by Czesław Miłosz and Leonard Nathan.
  (Modern European poetry series)
  1. Wat, Aleksander—Translations, English.
I. Miłosz, Czesław. II. Nathan, Leonard, 1924– .
III. Title. IV. Series.
PG7158.W28A25 1989   891.8'517—dc19   88-7692

ISBN 0-88001-183-1 (cloth)
ISBN 0-88001-184-X (paper)

*Frontispiece photo: Aleksander Wat with his grandson. Parc de Sceaux, 1967.
Courtesy of Paulina Wat.*

The text of this book is set in Bodoni Book.
Designed by Jody Hanson.

CONTENTS

7   Introduction

I

15   To Be a Mouse
16   Arithmetic
17   Before a Weimar Portrait of Dürer
19   A Flamingo's Dream
20   A Damned Man
22   Imagerie d'Épinal
23   Melodies from Hebrew
25   From Persian Parables
26   If the Word "Exists"
27   Before Breughel the Elder
29   Facing Bonnard
30   At the Exhibit
31   Poet
32   From Notes Written in Obory
33   A Recollection
35   Childhood of a Poet
36   Japanese Archery
38   A Joke
39   To a Roman, My Friend

40	Paris Revisited
42	In a Bar, Somewhere near Sevrès-Babylone
44	***

II

47	Songs of a Wanderer
62	Dreams from the Shore of the Mediterranean

III

79	Ode II
81	Ode III
84	A Turtle from Oxford
88	Taking a Walk
90	Farewell to Summer
91	An Attempt to Describe the Last Skirmish of the Second World War
93	***
94	From a Basket
95	In a Literary Café
96	From Hesiod
98	To Leopold Labedz
99	The Bride
101	A Dialogue on Wat Between Czeslaw Milosz and Leonard Nathan

INTRODUCTION

If the poetry of Central Europe has a place in the body of world poetry of this century (and it seems it does), Wat's poems deserve to be translated from their original Polish. This was my motivation in making them known to the English reader, though I was also acting out of loyalty to the memory of a friend.

Aleksander Wat, a shortened version of his family name, Chwat, was born in Warsaw on May 1, 1900. His family represented well the Polish-Jewish intelligentsia at the turn of the century, living between two traditions and two epochs. On the one hand there was a veneration of ancestors, rabbis, scholars, commentators of the Sacred Books; on the other, the new world of positivistic science and politics. Aleksander's father was a pious man and a student of the Kabbalah but also of Plotinus and Kierkegaard. He made no effort to try to influence the beliefs of his six children, and none received a religious education. The home was full of books in various languages and the children were well-read in Polish literature, learned French at an early age, and in school, Russian. Such an upbringing inclined them toward art and philosophy, in politics toward socialism. One of Aleksander's sisters became a famous actress in Warsaw, one brother became a painter. As a child Aleksander received his first initiation into poetry through the lullabies, nursery rhymes, and folk riddles he heard from Anna Mikulak, a beloved family servant. A pious woman, she used to take Aleksander with her to Roman Catholic churches—thus his lifelong fascination with Christianity and the Catholic ritual.

In 1917 he began to study philosophy at the University of Warsaw, surprising his professors with his thorough knowledge of Schopenhauer's works. At the same time he cofounded a Futurist writing group, and in 1919 he published his first volume of poems under the provocative title *Me from One Side and Me from the Other Side of My Pug-Iron Stove.* Many years later he recognized the Dadaist experimentation in those poems. At the time of their publication his poems were considered an oddity and no literary critic would treat them seriously. The predominant poetic school was Skamander, a group of talented young poets whose main concern was the discipline of the language. Wat was attempting to abolish syntax from his poetry; he seemed out of step with his time.

After that debut Wat for many decades was not active as a poet. His next volume of poetry appeared in 1957. Thus, he is a rare example of a poet whose finest achievement falls on his old age.

What happened in his life and in his intellectual biography in the meantime? His thought was centered around the crisis of European civilization, which by 1918 had found itself in ruins but was pretending to continue its existence as if unaware of the catastrophe. Values had lost their foundation and their meaning, and in his early poems Wat wanted to convey the idea that the ordered structures of the language were no longer adequate to this new state of things. He wanted to "dance on the ruins." A similar design is visible in his short stories written in the twenties and gathered in *Lucifer Unemployed* (*Bezrobotny Lucyfer,* 1927). These are mocking "dialectical" parables not unrelated to a modernistic trend in the prose of Yevgeny Zamyatin, early Ilya Ehrenburg, and Karel Čapek. In his memoirs Wat sees in these parables a nihilism at work that consisted of turning accepted values and notions upside down. He explains his next step as the result of his having reached a philosophical dead end and of subsequent despair. There seemed only one alternative: commitment to Communism; in this, he seemed to follow the same logic as did many European intellectuals, particularly in the neighboring Weimar Republic of Germany. Though never a member of the Communist Party, he edited in the years 1929–1932 the most important Polish Communist periodical, *The Literary Monthly (Miesięcznik Literacki),* heavily censored but somehow tolerated by the authorities. Wat proved to be an excellent, energetic, and resourceful editor able to reach a wide audience. During this time he made friends with Soviet writers on their trips to the West, particularly with Vladimir Mayakovsky, who visited Warsaw twice. In 1928 Wat himself traveled to Germany, where he met several German writers of the left, and to France, where he joined his

companion in the Polish Futurist movement, Bruno Jasieński.
Jasieński, leaning then toward Communism, wrote a "prophetic"
anticapitalist novel, *Je brûle Paris,* published in installments by
L'Humanité, for which he was expelled from France; he then went
to the Soviet Union, where he made a fantastic career as one of
the first writers introducing socialist realism into literature. He
died in a gulag near Vladivostok in 1939 or 1940, and should be
mentioned in this brief introduction, as he appears often in Wat's
poems.

The Literary Monthly was shut down by the authorities in
1932 and Wat spent a few months in prison, in rather
comfortable circumstances compared with those of his later Soviet
jails. In spite of his leftism, a large publishing house, Gebethner
and Wolff, made him its literary director and he worked in that
capacity until 1939.

On September 1 of that year Hitler attacked Poland. Wat, as
did many of his colleagues, escaped to the zone occupied by the
Soviet army in fulfillment of the pact Stalin and Hitler had
concluded on August 23, 1939. In January 1940, he was arrested
and passed through several prisons, including Lubianka in
Moscow. His interrogators tried to make him confess that he was
a Trotskyite, a Zionist, and also, when the mood struck them, an
agent of the Vatican. During his imprisonment he lost all track of
his wife and child. As he discovered later, they had been deported
to Soviet Asia soon after his imprisonment.

In summer 1941, after the outbreak of war between Germany
and Russia, he was transferred to a prison in Saratov, where he
spent a few months in a state close to starvation. As a result of
the amnesty for prisoners of Polish nationality, he was released
and arrived in Alma-Ata, Kazakhstan, frantically searching
everywhere for his lost family.

Many Russian writers evacuated from Moscow lived in
Alma-Ata, where the studios of Mosfilm had been transferred. Wat
was befriended and helped by Victor Shklovsky. He attended
discussions of a circle that counted among its members Mikhail
Zoshchenko and the film director Sergei Eisenstein. At last Wat
was reunited with his family, who had survived in a kolkhoz on
the Asian steppe. In 1943, as the relations between the Polish

government in exile and the Soviet Union worsened, the Wats were expelled from Alma-Ata to a little settlement in the desert, Ili. During the so-called "passportization" they refused to relinquish their Polish citizenship and were imprisoned. Wat was thrown in among the worst common-law criminals. They were supposed to beat him into obedience, but their chief, an eminent bandit, took him under his protection and Wat suffered no harm.

In 1946 the Wat family succeeded in returning to Poland. At that time the country was under the so-called coalition government and Wat renewed his literary activity, but in 1949, after the Communist Party had taken monopolistic power, he was silenced again. Branded "a hostile element," ostracized by his colleagues, he suffered a stroke and never recovered from its consequences—damage to some brain cells, which led to attacks of acute pain. Neurology clinics are the setting of several of his poems from the years 1950–1955. In 1956, the year of the "thaw," he returned to poetry in a renewal of creative vitality. With few exceptions his poems of maturity were written in the late 1950s and the 1960s. A change of political conditions brought about the publication of his *Poems (Wiersze)* in 1957. He was extolled, awarded prizes, asked forgiveness for having been persecuted. Now able to travel abroad, he looked for regions with a more hospitable climate, both geographically and figuratively, and lived mostly in southern France and Italy.

Wat's connection with Communism in his youth and his stay in the Soviet Union were for him the crucial experiences of his life. He constantly searched for a philosophical key to the phenomenon of the Soviet system and he planned to write a huge autobiographical book on the subject. Some of his friends, especially the late Professor Gleb Struve of the University of California at Berkeley, were instrumental in inviting him to Berkeley as a fellow of the Center for Slavic and East European Studies. They thought this would give him time to write and hoped that the mild California winters would be good for his health. The Wats spent one and a half years in Berkeley; they arrived at the end of 1963 and returned to France in the summer of 1965. Wat's health was poor and he couldn't work on his writings as he planned and this drove him to desperation. The tape recordings of my interviews with him, initiated as a therapeutic measure (the idea was Professor Gregory Grossman's) grew into Wat's main oeuvre in prose, a spoken memoir, *My Century (Mój wiek)*. It is an odyssey of a European intellectual through loyalties, ideas, prisons, hospitals, deportations, always in an effort to go deeper than the surface of the political events of the epoch he witnessed. The book consists of long monologues; I was mostly a listener, spellbound by his narrative.

Wat died in 1967 in Paris. His collected poems, whose title can be roughly rendered as *Dark Tinsel (Ciemne świecidło)*, were published in Paris in 1968. The preparation of *My Century* for print took his widow, Paulina Wat, many years, and when the voluminous book appeared (Polonia Book Fund Ltd, London, 1977) it was immediately hailed as a classic by Polish readers both in Poland and abroad. The second edition followed in 1981. The English version was published by the University of California Press (Berkeley, 1988), and the French version is to follow.

The Futurist movement in Poland was short-lived and produced no important poems. It stood apart even from a larger trend, the Avant-Garde, which in the twenties and thirties opposed the dominant group, Skamander; Polish poetry was thus divided into two camps. The Avant-Garde, evolving toward a specific, very rationalistic constructivism, moved away from the sonority, the metrical patterns, and the rhyme of its rivals while at the same time introducing its own rigors of "free verse." As a result of these developments in the period between the wars, Polish poetry acquired considerable freedom in versification and Wat's poems do not surprise by their "free" form. He uses lines of various lengths, occasionally rhyme, but he always shrugged at the Avant-Garde's pedantic programs and recognized the talents of the Skamander poets.

By defining himself as a Dadaist rather than a Futurist in his youth Wat wanted to point out a chaos of terms and labels common around 1920. In fact, whoever turned against the past in art and literature was often called a Futurist. But this term, when so used, did not signify a real affinity with more crystallized trends like Italian or Russian Futurism. To smash the language into pulp, to fragmentize words so that their syllables make a new idiom of, as Wat would say, one's naked skin—such a practice was much closer to the anarchism of Dada. But it would be premature to relegate such tendencies—and with them Wat's early poems—to a museum as part of the history of Modernism. An interesting Polish poet who made his debut after World War II, Miron Białoszewski, quite consciously exploited the possibilities of language as pulp, and we can only wonder whether this was not another poetic response to the ruins, much like that of a few decades earlier. In any case, Wat was pleased to learn that Białoszewski knew and valued his little volume *Me from One Side and Me from the Other Side of My Pug-Iron Stove.*

Several years ago I edited a collection of Wat's *Mediterranean Poems* (Ardis, 1977). These poems were translations done mostly by me with the help of my students. Together with Leonard Nathan I have revised that edition and we have added a number of poems in our joint translation. Thus, unless marked otherwise, the texts should be ascribed to our collaboration.

—CZESLAW MILOSZ

I

TO BE A MOUSE

To be a mouse. Preferably a field mouse. Or a garden mouse—
but not the kind that live in houses.
Man exudes an abominable smell!
We all know it—birds, crabs, rats.
He provokes disgust and fear.
     Trembling.

To feed on wisteria blossoms, on the bark of palm trees,
to dig up roots in cold, humid soil
and to dance after a brisk night. To look at the full moon,
to reflect in one's eyes the sleek light of lunar
     agony.

To burrow in a mouse hole against the time when wicked Boreas
will search for me with his cold, bony fingers
so he can squeeze my little heart under the
                        blade of his claw,

a cowardly mouse heart—
     a palpitating crystal.

Menton-Garavan, April 1956

ARITHMETIC

When you are alone
don't think you are alone.
He (she) is always with you.

Anywhere you go
you are followed.
The most faithful dog is not as faithful,
a shadow sometimes disappears,
he (she)—never.

That red-headed whore loafs in the entrance of a hotel
and with her is—not her double—she, another she.
That old man sneaks in after her like a cat
and with him, his inseparable companion.

Those two on a bed in contortions.
These two sit at the foot and wait, sadly bowing their heads.

Paris, June 1956

BEFORE A WEIMAR PORTRAIT OF DÜRER

(In two versions)

    1.

Terror turns your flesh green
when you wake up at night. In order to meet fear proudly
you stand naked before the mirror, a candle in your hand,
every fiber of your body freezes with fear.

How awful it is to meet your own image at night,
when it wakes you at night: "Here," it calls, "here, kitty."
And then with brutal abruptness: "Back!"
Like a sergeant to a new recruit who hoped to escape the battlefield.
                                                                                                In vain.

Furnaces are already lit, smoke ascends to heaven.
                                           "Back,"
the sergeant orders. And you know he calls you nowhere,
                                                                     to nothingness.
Which is a tangle of horrors
lifting the hair on the head of a pre-archaic Medusa.

    2.

"From where?"—"From death."—"Where to?"—"To death."
"And you?"—"From life. To life."
"Who are you?"—"I am You.
As in a mirror:
you are my reflection.
Or the other way round."
—"How to determine who is a reflection of whom?"
—"You won't tell that. There is no mirror."
There is no mirror. And yet I see my body, terrified,
bathed in slowly streaming tremors of fear,
lit by the liturgical green of a candle.

There is no mirror. There is only this spell.
There is only an echo which does not know whose echo it is,
whether it is even an echo of somebody at all?
It has always heard only its own voice,
it is always reborn out of itself, a wondrous Phoenix,
eternal parthenogenesis of phenomena.
Where to? To death. Where to? To life.
There is only I, but life does not know whose it is either.
Whether of somebody?
And hope? Oh yes, it makes itself heard, like a bird at night,
when all voices are silent, when everything sleeps,
when everything has died and all hopes are extinguished.

A FLAMINGO'S DREAM

Water water water. And nothing but water.
If only one inch of land! An inch of no-matter-what land!
To set foot on! Just an inch!

We begged the gods for that! All of them!
Water gods, land gods, southern gods, northern gods,
For an inch, a strip, a scrap of any kind of land!
No more than just enough to support the claw of one foot!
And nothing. Only water. Nothing except water.
Water water water.
If only a speck of land!
There is no salvation.

A DAMNED MAN

The first thing to appear in my dream was a coffee mill.
Most ordinary. The old-fashioned kind. A coffee-brown color.
(As a child, I liked to slide open the lid, peek in and instantly
snap it shut. With fear and trembling! So that my
                                        teeth chattered with terror.
It was as if I myself were being ground up in there! I always knew
I would come to a bad end!)
So first there was a coffee mill.
Or perhaps I only imagined it, because a moment later
                                        a windmill stood there.
And that windmill stood on the sea,
                    on the horizon's line, at its very center.
Its four wings creaked and cracked as they turned. They
                    were probably grinding somebody up.
And at the tip of every one of them
an equilibrist in white
revolved to the melody of *The Merry Widow.*
Supported by his left hand resting on the wing, he
                              floated, fiery, fluid,
a silver flame tapping its feet in the ether.
Then he waned. And so one after the other. It would have
                    been dark if not for a burning moon.
Where did they come from? Girls on horseback. My
                    marvelous equestriennes!
Lightly on heavy but swift Percherons
they gallop one after another and I see crowds, crowds of them—
some in ruffles of tulle, others, naked, stark naked
                              in black silk stockings,
still others in beads—golden, turquoise, black and iridescent,
and their thighs white like sugar! Like teeth! And
                    strong, O mighty God, how strong!
(As a young boy I dreamt: girl on horseback—only an
     equestrienne
will saddle the great love in my life! Well, I've never met one.

And it's probably better that way, for what a couple we would
                              have made: a girl on horseback
and a bookkeeper in a nationalized funeral parlor.)
Well, nothing lasts forever. Since a moment later
instead of those girls, Sabines were parading, armored
                         women, much more vulgar after all
(eleven years ago I fell in love with a certain Sabina,
a divorcee, alas without reciprocity).
Thus the Sabines
not ravished, but, let me concede, ravishing. Taking me where?
Where? How can I know where?
In any case—toward annihilation.

I woke up. I always knew I would come to a bad end.

IMAGERIE D'ÉPINAL

(On the death of Reik, Slansky and thousands of others)

The executioner yawned. The blood was still dripping from his axe.
"Don't cry, my child, don't, here's a lollipop."

He took her in his arms. Stroked her. And she
                                        stared at the head.
At the sightless eyes. At the dumb lips.

It was her father's head. Later on, embalmed,
washed, it was stuck on a pole and prettily painted.

With that pole she marched in a parade on a sunny, populous road,
under her school placard:
                    "Happiness for all—to enemies death."

1949

MELODIES FROM HEBREW

1.

To these old Roman arches
Came a Jew from the ghetto.
   —LENARTOWICZ

I strived to reach you
from early childhood
O beautiful and mighty
triumphal
gate of Titus!

Lost in the middle of the obscure path of life
in a labyrinth of jails and hospital rooms
I dreamt of you
beautiful and mighty,
of eternal Rome,
triumphant
gate of Titus!

But when I stood before you, gate of Titus
—O horrible! O shameful!—
I saw
carved in stone
the face of my father.
his shoulders bent
under a holy menorah!
His hands shackled
with your chains!
His eyes exhausted,
eyes attesting to
incessant rebellion,
eternal hatred
for you, triumphant,
now defeated,
pagan Rome!

I will not walk
I will not walk
O my Judean sisters
I will not walk under the Arch of Titus.*

Rome, 1949

*Until the creation of the State of Israel Roman Jews would not walk under the Arch of Titus. (A.W.)

2.

*In their shade harpists are sitting and rocking their heads
in their withered palms . . .*
—KORNEL UJEJSKI

On the Babylonian shores we were sitting, exhausted.
"Sing!"—the guards were shouting—
"Now we sing, and sing lively
a war song of Zion and a mournful hymn to Yahveh.
Let the music of slaves caress our ears!"

We would sing—
were our song a poison!
We would sing—
were its words a dagger!
We would sing—
were our song a curse—
and not a joy, not freedom, not a blessing!
What do they know of Yahveh, Baal's worshippers,
what do they know of the sweet pith of Zion's songs!
And there were among us those who sang for the strangers.
The Just Lord struck their lips dumb with leprosy,
their harps are smashed, their candelabra trampled into dust
and their houses shamed by dereliction.

1956

FROM PERSIAN PARABLES

By great, swift waters
on a stony bank
a human skull lay shouting:
Allah la ilah.

And in that shout such horror
and such supplication
so great was its despair
that I asked the helmsman:

What is there left to cry for? Why is it still afraid?
What divine judgment could strike it again?

Suddenly a rising wave
took hold of the skull
and tossing it about
smashed it against the bank.

Nothing is ever over
—the helmsman's voice was hollow—
and there is no bottom to evil.

IF THE WORD "EXISTS"

If the word "exists" is to have meaning
it should indicate something we can return to.
Yet there is no return! Everything is once
and before it has begun to "exist," it has already ceased to "exist"
(Notice: "has begun" and "has ceased" are equally unfounded)
and the alternation "is" and "is not" is not a sequence of time,
it unfolds itself beyond time—insofar as "unfolds"
can be used here.
Therefore,
let us return to essence. For with it we are more certain.
Since we create it ourselves. It is not dependent
on whether it "is" or on whether it "is not."

How good it is to return to old rejected concepts!
(N.B. The meaning of that "let us return" is
                                         common. So, for example,
Odysseus returned to Penelope, to her who knew the secret:
that one must weave and unweave. And again weave and unweave.)

BEFORE BREUGHEL THE ELDER

Work is a blessing,
I tell you that, I—a professional loafer!
Who bedded down in so many prisons! Fourteen!
And in so many hospitals! Ten! And innumerable hotels!
Work is a blessing.
How else could we deal with the lava of fratricidal love
                                      toward our fellow men?
With those storms of extermination of all by all?
With brutality that has no bottom, no measure?
With the black-and-white era which does not want to end,
endlessly repeating itself da capo like a record
forgotten on a turntable,
spinning by itself?
Or perhaps someone invisible watches over the phonograph?
    Horror!
How, if not for work, could we live in the paradise of
                                    social hygienists
who never dip their hands in blood without antiseptic gloves?
Horror!
How else could we cope with death?
That Siamese twin sister of life
who grows together with it—in us, and is extinguished with it
and surely for that reason is ineffective.
And so we have to live without end,
without end. Horror!
How, if not for work, could we cope with ineffective death
(Don't scoff!)
which is like a sea,
where everyone is an Icarus, one of nearly three billion,
and besides, so much happens all around us
and everything is equally unimportant, yes, unimportant
although so difficult, so inhumanly difficult, so painful!
How then could we cope with all that?

Work is our rescue.
I tell you that—I, Pieter Breughel, the Elder (and even I, your modest servant, Wat, Aleksander)—work is our rescue.

Saint-Mandé, July 1956

FACING BONNARD

Blond light blew away grayness, shadows, mists
from a body that left the bathtub and does not yet go to the
    coffin.
The body is tawny, flame-spotted, and the bathtub, rosy,
    flesh-colored.
And the coffin? As usual with a coffin: dimly purple.
(Besides, the coffin's not visible: its colors suffice).
That translation from our world, don't ask whether faithful,
gives pleasure to the eye. The other senses are mum.
But to the eye it gives pleasure. That's enough. Quite.
Be patient. Wait. You will see how that pleasure
opens up as an egg of dream-meditation.
Our artist enclosed in it a ballet of possibilities
where he himself—and you—are both an observer and an author,
a corps de ballet, surely, but also a true soloist.

AT THE EXHIBIT

Our world. So small
that one guitar
is enough
to populate it with sounds—
if played by Love.

Love is not seen
though it is present.

Beside the guitar a patera with apples
—a mark of royalty
known from the tarot;
the realization of evil-good;
the fruit of the Hesperides
but not made of gold,
on the contrary—of colors
from our world
which is so small
that one guitar is enough
etc.

All this is seen
except Love
which is not seen
though it is present
in a small exhibit
of a picture dealer
on Faubourg Saint-Honoré.

Paris, December 1955

POET

Is the poet, I thought, the one who, uninvited,
came to the feast of the Philistines?
And stood there, at the head of the table,
his hair piled up as a helmet.
Oh, how he towers over the council of armed Philistines!
He arrives from the lands where none of them wandered
and never will.
Where the final things clash against each other
and break like icebergs
and sink
or float away
toward new risings and settings of the sun,
which no one of them will see.
He could have carried before him his scorn like two torches—
but he ignited love in one eye,
in the other, anger.
He could have, out of birds steaming on golden platters,
prophesied their triumph or defeat. Defeat, multiple defeat.
He could have yelped and with his stony fist
split in half bronze armor.
For he arrived and yet refused to be invited. . . . Or
he could have charmed himself into a white teal
and by one movement of wings
soared away, then falling stonelike down
on black waters
on carmine waves
of Styx. . . . Or, or
on pure waters
native
distant.

FROM NOTES WRITTEN IN OBORY

X was asked
     if he believed in the objective existence of Parzota
—To believe in the objective existence of Parzota—
     that smacks of mysticism,
I am an old horse, you know, and a staunch
rationalist—
answered X.
The sequel was more interesting.

X persisted in his refusal to believe in the
                          objective existence of
     Parzota.
Who, the said Parzota, put him in a dungeon,
                          tortured him.
Yet everything would have been in perfect order
if not for one sad circumstance:
the stupid man of principle was so obstinate that
                          he died in the dungeon:
Poor Parzota! he will never know,
Sentenced as he was to eternal doubt
Whether he had objective existence.

A RECOLLECTION

Precisely in the same place, long ago: thirty years,
I left him, very young. Fascinated
he looked at Saint-Étienne-du-Mont. Shaken by the discovery
of its hidden identity with what he guessed in himself,
yet not in a flash of vision, but in persistent labor,
in an act of strenuous penetration
that Husserl calls eidetic intuition—

he absorbed thus the massif articulated in black-gray,
the orphic play of lights on it, the incantation of graph,
the sequence of planes,
the module and rhythm of solids, the concise counterpoint,
prisoner of ancient stone.

He plunged into mute music of intricate architecture,
similar to a melomane who, listening to an orchestra,
studies the score and does not know whether he hears symbols
or sees a harmony of sounds suddenly made visible.

Thus he stood leaning against the wall, by Sainte-Géneviève,
from where he had slipped out, to exchange the signs
mean, ambiguous, for others—clear and certain.
To read from those walls the key of light of each hour,
to discover volume, color, weight and charm of space—
to discover himself in it! . . . To grasp, comprehend and judge!

Here I left him then—I, his prodigal shadow.
After ranging through cities and mainlands, going as far as the
    Pamir,
wallowing in miseries, in defeats and sorrows,
here I came to find him. . . .
                  Oh, to return to him, return!
I look around the piazza. He is not there.

There is no return.
>   *L'infinita venuta del tutto* is an illusion.
Nobody is here. Only strange people
>   hurrying after their strange affairs.

CHILDHOOD OF A POET

Melos whispered words in his ear,
their meaning was incomprehensible.
Weaving them by twos, by threes
she would crown his forehead
with thorns.

She fed his heart with bitterness.
Till, overflowing with nausea, it exploded in a spasm
of joy
shared with nobody
nobody
nobody.

That was a sad childhood.
Sounds, remembrances, dreams
in which he always soared one inch above earth.
Then he fell.
The fall of a child . . .
The levitation of a poet.

JAPANESE ARCHERY

I

The hand tells the bowstring:
    Obey me.

The bowstring answers the hand:
    Draw valiantly.

The bowstring tells the arrow:
    O arrow, fly.

The arrow answers the bowstring:
    Speed my flight.

The arrow tells the target:
    Be my light.

The target answers the arrow:
    Love me.

II

The target tells arrow, bowstring, hand and eye:
    Tat twam asi.

Which means in a sacred tongue:
    I am Thou.

III

(Footnote of a Christian:
    O Mother of God,

watch over the target, the bow, the arrow
    and the archer).

Translated by Richard Lourie

A JOKE

TO GORDON CRAIG

Bunches of carnations in a tin pitcher.
Beyond the window, is that a faun playing a flute?
In a fusty room the semi-darkness of dawn.
The lovers sleep. On the sill

the cat purrs. In its dream a rabble of birds.
She wakens like a bird and, trembling,
opens her eye on the alabaster
shaded mournfully by her streaming hair.

She found in it her wreath fished up from a river
and searches for his hand, looking for protection.
Then plunges into sleep again—into a flow, a flow . . .

Suddenly the door creaked softly. Somebody enters. Surprised.
Looks, hardly believes: My son—with a woman!
and retreats on tiptoe: O Hamlet! Hamlet!

Venice, September 1956

TO A ROMAN, MY FRIEND

Everything that lies in rubble
reaches tenderly at me:
the ruins of my Warsaw
the ruins of your Rome.

In April 'forty-six
I saw two old goats
searching for some special herbs
in the former Albrecht's Café
(now overgrown with nettles,
thistles, burdock, spear grass).
Their barefoot shepherdess
in graveyard stillness
stood gaping, a child, under a pathetic column that once adorned
    the fourth floor
                           of the Credit Society building,
where then it was just a fancy ornament
changed today into an orphaned pendicle
on a fragment of charred wall.

On the Aventino I met two goats, roamers of ruins,
and a barefoot shepherdess
staring at faded frescoes.

Thus after man's glory,
after his acts and disasters
goats arrive. Smelly,
comic and worthy goats
to search among remnants of glory
for medicinal herbs and forage
for earthly nourishment.

PARIS REVISITED

At every new return
my first day in this city—
like the first day of creation:
and I see, I see that it's good.

Here a thousand voices
sound reveille to life!
The memory of places sings,
a pathetic *cantatrice*—
and her voice is not getting old
and her echo never fades
refracted from venerable stones
in eternal repetition
ever the same, not the same,
live, never dying,
woven into a frivolous
tune in the street.

Here a thousand voices
sound reveille to life!
Call and forbid you to die!
Summon, restore to life!
A thousand lips entice you!
A thousand charms cast spells:
fulgurant reason
in eyes met by chance,
a smile that opens lips
like a flower after the night,
sweet tenderness of the air
in the avenue of trimmed chestnuts,
a call of a wandering tune
and the smell of earthly foods
and a rainbow on the pavement

of an old church across the square . . .
And a young man's faded shadow
who—so long ago!—was discovering
this world for the first time.

Here a thousand voices
sound reveille to life!
Rise from the dead,
son of misfortune!
Bow humbly to this land,
kiss the callused hand
of the old city of Paris.

IN A BAR, SOMEWHERE NEAR SEVRÈS-BABYLONE

(From Parisian kitsch)

A slut was sitting at the counter. She kept her eyes fixed
on a glass from which she sucked through a straw, a ruby liquor.
Not very young, but not old. Sturdy. Brutal features,
yet character dressed them in dignity, even nobility.
It was still winter. The morning was marvelous, sunny.
Paris untangled itself from iridescent aquamarine mist.
In the window a little church across the square. Where bells
                                    happened to be chiming.
I do not know for what reason.

The woman raised her eyelids. Like a ballerina
who rises on her toes. But her dun-yellow pupils
were petrified. And yet they concealed inside
a flicker or perhaps a light—
a light imprisoned in amber.
This made her resemble a Cumaean sibyl
seated on a stool at a counter, her legs spread.

She swept the room with a casually professional look,
sized up two old men bent over dominoes
and hesitated suddenly when meeting my eyes—
uncertain whether I would be a timid aspirant
to her breasts, hard and robust, to her legs, chopped out of stone,
in black openwork fin-de-siècle stockings.
(Where did she find them in our era of nylon,
she a model of Toulouse-Lautrec's,
a Babylonian whore?)

But soon recognized her mistake, slowly retracted her eyes,
covered them with thick eyelids as with a lampshade of tin.
And again fixed her pupils on the very tall glass
from which she sucked through a straw blood-ruby liquor.
The bells of the little church chimed more and more insistently,
my face in a mirror looked at me, here somewhat alien, not mine.

Two big cats walked in from the street through the half-open door,
step by step following each other, stalking cautiously, slowly—
both fat and dirty gray. Swinging their tails in rhythm
as soldiers in a parade swing their arms, unaware of onlookers.
They came up to the woman, rubbed against her legs,
then lazily lay down on both sides of the tabouret—
you would say: two drowsy sphinxes on guard at a sullen tomb.

The tightness left her petrified face.
To relax.
That was an instant of happiness.

* * *

TO PAUL ÉLUARD

Leaves whirl, leaves swirl,
leaves torn from Auschwitz trees.
Leaves in a gold-gray windstorm
leaves torn off leaves stripped off
leaves hacked flogged
gassed charred
leaves kneeling leaves screaming
leaves raising a lament to heaven!

My eyes stricken by terrible leaves,
they confuse my steps, turn me
they turn and darken, leaves, leaves
till I fall down
tangled in leaves
in leafing darkness!

Oh, close your eyes, sleepy Kore
who repose on your bed,
flayed and bloodless.
O lute of my sighs, be silent, be silent!
O close your eyes, buried
by leaves from Auschwitz.

April 1946

II

SONGS OF A WANDERER

Ich stech das Licht. Ich stech das Licht. Ich stech das Herz das ich liebe.
—SCHÖNWERTH, *Aus der Oberplatz: Sitten und Sagen*

I

For whom is the garden fated?
Who is happy there?
Whose eyes will be my haven?
Someone steals toward me.
What falls in the abyss?
A scream resounds.
A hand gropes upward.
Give me your hand, my son.
Wife, look into my eyes.

II

Disgusted by everything alive I withdrew into the stone world: here
I thought, liberated, I would observe from above, but
 without pride, those things
tangled in chaos. With the eyes of a stone, myself a stone among
 stones, and like them sensitive,
pulsating to the turning of the sun. Retreating into
 the depth of myself, a stone,
motionless, silent; growing cold; present through a waning
 of presence—in the cold
attractions of the moon. Like sand diminishing in
 an hourglass, evenly,
ceaselessly, uniformly, grain by grain. Thus I shall be subject
only to the rhythms of day and night. But—
no dance in them, no whirling, no frenzy: only
 monastic rule, and silence.
They do not become, they are. Nothing else. Nothing
 else, I thought, loathing
all that becomes.

                        I, a stone among stones. Oh, never had I thought
of stone in the words of death. I had always felt in it
                                      a heart, a pulsing
of its life, and not just in its internal structures, which amaze
onlookers, photographers, mineralogists. . . . Simply:
                                      the heart of a stone: Simply:
the dreams of a stone. To be in the heart of a stone—
                                      how much I desired this!
In the heart of a stone, without the flaw which
                                      through our tainted veins
slushes deep into our hearts and grows, making them
                                      totally putrid matter,
subjected to all decay.
            The dreams of a stone! how I
                                      wanted to see the dreams
of a stone, through its own stony eyes! Perhaps
                                      a human child, an infant,
when it is no longer a palpitating sponge of flesh,
                                      but not yet—a man,
perhaps, in his eye, he retains a dream of a stone, not even a
      dream—
a reflection, an echo of a dream, distant and fading away. Oh,
how I wanted to be in the thought of a stone, to be what
                                      its thought thinks. Or—
cursed in the beginning, exiled from stone, how I wanted to touch
the thought of a stone, just as I touch rose petals,
                                      careful not to let it feel
my coarse, bulbous fingers, the fingers of a usurper:
it might die of disgust.
                  The thought of a stone, the thought of a
                                      rose, what if they were akin
in its very short season, when it is still wisdom, folded up,
and yet open to love? Eros, agape—as I call this
                                      in the obscure speech
of men, in speech without eyes, no—with eyes
                                      repeatedly gouged out;
in snail words sent in whispers toward our cannibal lips
by our brain, which is nourished with blood, subjected to
                                      rottenness, decay, putrescence,
contaminating everything in its grasp with putrescence, decay.

                   What's erosion, I thought,
to a stone? What's the crumbling of its inner structures?
                              The heart of a stone
is not in structures, in space-time relations, it is generous,
rebuilding structures, while time, impotent, disintegrates
                              them. The heart of a stone
does not submit to annihilation, to the death of everything
                    which becomes.
                              Armored,
it is a sovereign monad.
                    I didn't envy the stone the
                              riches of its inner world.
I did not look for a shell to hide in, to gorge my mollusk
                    senses on the food of colors.
What are riches to the stone? Yes, in riches we surpassed
stones during our million years' existence on earth. But
                              what are riches to them?
In their inner world nothing but poverty—as we call it,
                    using the gouged-out eyes
of our poor speech. But everything there is meaningful and pure,
                    everything there is everything.
Only there. If God exists, He is there. At the heart of stones.
                    Also—in their dreams.
          Even the tree, the most perfect
                    creation of the demiurge
just before he fell asleep, when he was dozing on the
                    same edge above which
nods the head of a schoolboy, tired from poring over
                    a book on the table,
on that edge from which something irresistibly pulls us down, into
                    the dark, down into the dark
from where we rose and rise obstinately—even the tree, I say
     again,
when, like a strong man, it wedges into the stone and splits it
     apart
with its savage, dirt-covered, worm-covered root; when it
                    pulls out of Mother Earth
and shamelessly brings to light her magic dreams:
                    leaves, birds, seeds,
even the tree, always prepared for flights, vibration,

                        frenzy—even the tree—
I say again, the most beautiful creation of the demiurge
                        while on the edge of sleep—
what can it do to the stone?
            Perhaps, in a blink of marveling,
the wildest creature, in whom was set the terrifying spark of
    genius,
so desiring to die out! so unhappy is it in that dwelling place—
                        perhaps man in marveling
has a flash of intuition, when he approaches stones with pain,
                        but, silently, without pride?—
a sculptor whose chisel, already lifted, is held back
                        by the voice of the stone:
Stop, here is your threshold, one scratch more and you will
                        be rejected inexorably,
without return.
                So I thought about stone. And
                        since I loved everything
that is not even the negation of stone—but worse: otherness, all,
that is subjected to flaws, transience, death and—
                        worse: resurrection
from death; and since I was sensuous to the marrow of my
    marrow,
since I loved my senses, my skin, all skin, every skin even unto
fiery hatred—the heart of a stone was closed to me,
sealed fast.
            But now is the time of old age. *Aetas*
                    serenitatis. Thus, disgusted
with the world of the living, its beauty turned toward
                        death, decaying, rising
from the dead as vermin, as acrid weeds, as manure
                        for peasant hands, thus
I fled into the stone world, in order—a stone among
                        stones, done with pride,
although from above—to close slowly my eyes, not yet
                        stony but no longer human,
to your sufferings, to your tenderness, to your
                        labors and those agonies
of yours, to all that is subjected to incessant putrefaction,
that is our torture, our shame, our shameful pity,

our beauty like radiant eyes in the face of a
                              hydrocephalic hunchback.

   III

So now, having fled into the stone world, I was slowly falling
                         asleep, a stone under
my head, feeling how the warmth of its heart penetrates my head,
and makes it similar, its twin; when on the
                         edge of sleep, from where,
heavy with darkness we lean into greater darkness—now,
                         when I dreamt there: I, too,
am a stone among stones, and, like them, I am exalted
                         but without pride, inert
and yet tense with strength, in a tense fullness which hangs
                         in the clenched stone fist
of the moon over a sterile landscape—
              I was awakened by the din of those
whom I survived.

                    Remember! Remember!
         Not in a double row did they surround me;
                              not in the carriage
of a survivor must I pass them; no holiday dresses do they wear:
no wreaths on their heads. Naked, though tightly
                         swathed in the lava
of clay. Like that man in Pompeii, who managed
                    to lower his brow
lifted in amazement and to fix his tired death-stare on the earth
which betrayed him.
                    Remember! Remember!—They shout: and
                         they want to be forgotten.
Remember!—They shout: and they want eternal oblivion. Our hell—
is in the memory of those who will survive us.
                    Driven out by the din and the sham
of those whom I survived, I walked down through
                         rubble. And having lost
everything I knew in that difficult descent, I am again what
I had been.

IV

It is not erosion which crumbles stone here.
                            But the jaws of an old woman, whom
I pass on the road. A patient old woman, her eyes like cinders
under a dark brown straw hat. What can atrophied jaws
crumble? Blind, this I see, but with her gnarled hand and
                                     her olive walking stick
she gropes for her son's return from work. All
                                        expectation. So dwarfed
you would swear: she comes from a workshop of olive-wood
                                     holy figures. And time
tarnished her with its patina. Thus she stands, on the
                                       domestic threshold, bent
double. The cold Mother Earth.
                          It is not erosion which crumbles stone
                                       here. For the rot
is in its nature. To rot, to scale off, to disintegrate: this
                                       is posited in the law
of minerals. In the law of mollusks. In the law of man.
                                     Obstinate olive trees
dug into the earth walls of these cliffs; and deep
                                     below—a vast trough.
It still holds at bay upsurging waves of mountains,
                                     once aroused against it
by the Vengeful Hand, when they were liquid, fiery,
                                     crested. And thus
they petrified almost hunchbacked, all in the same
crouch: henchmen waiting for the Master's sign.
The Vengeful Hand set them here as an eternal threat
above the mole and the bush, above the fretful ant,
                                   above the young human
species, which secretes the glue of labor. . . .
                        True, no man in sight: but,
smoke from the farms. But, hamlets. But, highways, roads,
                                   paths, in an incomprehensible
tangle. And—farther on—streams snake, coil in silver,
                                 and far, far away
the navigable sea, and from under its shiny skin,
                                   in this hour of luminescence

the skeletons of sunken ships project their afterflow. Oh yes,
water, also water, even water, so immaculate—
                              is contaminated, condemned;
for myriads of ages plasma crawls out of its floods,
                              in a relentless flow,
plasma a billion times mutilated. Trampled down.
                    Smashed. Desecrated.
So it is not erosion. Not erosion.
The old woman on the threshold of her house
bent double, all in expectation of her son's return from work
                    (he has a job in Grasse,
at Grasset's perfume factory).
          Smoke dear to one's nostrils,
          sun-drenched windowpanes,
          and you, my dear road—the vehicle
          for a return home.
          In lieblicher Bläue
          die Fenster wie die Thore
          der Schönheit . . . Dichterisch
          wohnet der Mensch auf dieser
Erde. . . . Cold Mother *Ziemla*. She waits
for her son's return. Who
waits for me? . . . Nobody in sight
except her.

          —*Salut à vous!*—she calls loudly
          and confidently. In this excellent
          echo chamber of the air.

Not erosion. Not hamlets, farms, fire trails, interlacing roads. But—
eczema. But—eczema of the earth, mycosis of the earth. Decrepitude
          of the earth. Processes of the earth's
disintegration. Black blight on a stone carcass. The scaling and
                    psoriasis of her scrofulous
child. Also water, even water—certainly—most of all! The digit
on a banknote delights the naive eye. But the
          experienced one sees the watermark: the mark
of eczema, the mark of decrepit nature, alive and not alive.
The old woman in a dark hat

stands on the threshold bent double
and in a pleasant voice sings:
>   *And I bore you, son, for eternal dying*
>   *And I raised you, son, for painful rest.*
And with her olive stick weaves a concise pattern in the air.

A stray sheep, staring at me: my worthy sheep, you will rot.
Manure, mycosis, rot, the agony of things living and not living.

    V

"Off with his head."
–THE QUEEN, from *Alice in Wonderland*

A pretty innkeeper of La Chèvre d'Or
sits on the porch, her fingers interlaced.
Both of us with a glass of light
wine.
         This trapezoidal
square. And a sycamore
in a casement. A fountain circa 1900,
ascending roads, descending roads
                        crisscrossed.
Along one soldiers descend,
along another soldiers ascend.
60 km., 20 kg. load,
Jean, Pierre, Jacques—and again
Pierre, Jean, Jacques. They march in single file,
one after another. Where are they being herded?
A rosy inn, yellow tables, sapphire pasture
and blue above our heads. A whiskered old lady
in a gray hat, her head—a toy block set squarely
on her belly (check to see what Roman artists called this
in the age of decline). She crossed obliquely and vanished.
                       Next a cat, young, fat.
Off with her head—shouts the Queen.
The poor soldiers droop under their gear,
wipe off sweat, chance upon the fountain circa 1900,
move out in single file, one of them stumbled,

sighed, farted, fell, his buddies roar,
a bellowing dissonance in a serene concert
of pastoral silence. Off with their heads,
shouts the innkeeper. You are pretty, innkeeper of Cabris,
when you play with your pretty dog Diane,
when you plunge your narrow fingers into her ragged hair,
when you tickle her under her floppy ear,
when your gaze drifts to the pasture
from where dignified, colorful village magi
descended three weeks ago on Epiphany.
                    Now from there a hunter without a leg—
he lost it in the war—a local Don Juan, is coming
for his daily *pastis.* In a smooth Aronde
Mister Fevrard drives up with his Parisian girlfriend.
A setter runs across the square in a chic trot. It scared off
a permanent resident, the cat. The owner of the gift shop
returns from her siesta, an ingratiating smile on her flat face.
A stout ninety-year-old villager dozes over a liter of red wine.
He breaks wind, the simple soul. Mister Fevrard moves
                        ten yards farther on.
And all this in the sun, *un après-midi d'hiver.*
38 C. In February, unthinkable
in my country! Where people are born, love, die
in ferocious February. February, wear thick boots
                        and be wary. My country
is a peasant country. In this peasant country
the beautiful innkeeper, a pearl in her ear,
reads Agatha Christie in the doorway. Bored by Diane,
by Agatha, too. In a red Peugeot
a laborer drives up with his heavy-boned family. And again
soldiers pass, one after another, then in pairs,
then in a crowd. How they reek. Of the long road,
and of health. How they will stink
in sickness, in agony. Diane
ran after the last one. Off,
off with his head, shouts Queen Diana Hecate
Luna. In the pallid firmament. A shepherd
with his sheep passes by. A cat—a brooding philosopher—
approaches, also the village drunkard, Monsieur Maxime,
a gentle drunkard, kind to people, eager for odd jobs,

slovenly, high school graduate, in an embroidered skullcap—
(What fate brought it here from the valleys of Fergana
where in the whiteness of snows are violet-colored
                                          mountains and the violet
of peaches by the violet of rocks, and the violet tenderly
                                      washed in the greens
of a stream, while a rider-philosopher,
a knight in tatters, girt with the scarlet
of Kashmir, passes by in a wild gallop, *la ilah ill Allah,* passes us
bent down to the dust under dun-colored bags from a
                                      labor camp?) And again,
God, those annoying soldiers.
                They see green,
                I see snows.
                They—in the young sun,
                I—in a ferocious winter.
                A hunter, a laborer, a bird, a village
                                  orchestra, it returns—
a moustached head, he flails the pavement with a
                                  scissor kick. Mister Fevrard
gets into the car with his Parisian girlfriend. Off with his head,
shouts the innkeeper.
                Whose head? I look around.
Mister Fevrard drove off with his Parisian girlfriend.
Nobody. Alone on the square. With you. Only
                                    with you. Always with you.
Off!—no! No, it happened differently.

VI

Ah! Seigneur! Donnez-moi la force et le courage
De contempler mon coeur et mon corps sans dégoût.
        —BAUDELAIRE, *Un Voyage à Cythere*

It happened quite differently.
As it does among people. Warmly. Gemütlich. In this way:
Three good buddies, around a samovar with vodka and
    cucumbers.
Two in suspenders; one in socks, another in slippers,

and the third as if dressed for a ball: a tie, cheap pin-striped
trousers, a frock coat of heavy fabric, lacquered shoes.
> *Let the majordomo rage,*
> *the lackey's looking grim:*
> *we've got you locked up in our cage,*
> *we'll tear you limb from limb*

—they sing in chorus, the first even has a quite nice tenor.
They drink, belch, look through
dossier after dossier, piles of dossiers.
"Whore and bandit," scribbles the one in gray socks;
"Off with his head," adds another:
"and brand him as a brigand," the one in the tie writes
in a fine hand, like a worthy lawyer.
"A machine of hell?! A masterpiece of Satan?!"—let
the morons unravel it. And we here in a warm stench,
yawning, scratching ourselves, over cucumbers and a samovar—
three buddies. Off— — —
Off!—a voice in the air cries
without lips. —"Whose?"—"A head!"
It is no more. Chopped off. Let's go back.
The wind from the sea
gathers us up. And wisps of smoke are fragrant. In the air
pure as a tear. How far one can see! How
tender are the little lights of men,
amen.
> The green hunter
> with a vigilant barrel
> with a deaf-mute dog
> at his post.
> Don't ask who. I've known
> for a long time.

VII

Satan—and not the Evil one. The Evil one is a devil,
Behemoth, Azazel. No crony to Satan,
not at all, neither kith nor kin.
The other rebelled, yes, but he was rebelling
out of concern for man. Man, it has a proud ring to it,

that's why we rot in this hole, just our tough luck.
As to the devil, he runs errands for God, see
Job 1, 12. From which you should not conclude
God is Evil. On the contrary—Infinitely, Incomprehensibly Good,
which is only a vulgar metaphor of the Incomprehensibly Good, as
it was justly written by Saint Dionysius,
the one who had his head cut off.
So don't ask: *Unde malum?* Evil is apprehended Good. Perhaps
the reverse. Anyhow, a Good at a lower, so to speak,
stage of *Development*. Why is Satan identified with the devil?—
How should I know? A riddle, at least, at our stage, of
                                            people in the clink. That's
why we are locked up. Our tough luck. Besides, ask
                                            Schaff. From the divine
point of view we must be locked up as the spawn of
                                            Satan. From the human,
as children of the devil. Confused, as usual, like
                                            philosophers. But anyhow—
in the clink.

VIII

I play *la pétanque*. I swear obscenely.
Dominoes with my cronies, backgammon.
I prattle. Grow muddy with drinks. Covered
with sweat, yes, sweat, eczema, mycosis.
My clothes are filthy. No fragrant oils
from Grasse will help; not all the perfumes of Arabia
                                            can clean them. Nor
will the breath of my little sister mimosa under the window
undo anything. The sun
looses a parasite in my hair. In its pincers
the tightly caught bone creaks like an old piece of furniture.
It is a high note. It tears heaven apart
from the west to the east. In vain. Nothing
will reach out of there. The Hand is no more. A stone which
does not fall. Hurry up, you gypsy soul. The night
                                            is near. Centauresses
defending the Throne, as I wrote at the age of twenty.

                    Centauresses are no more.
Soon, the screech of an owl. The Hunter is already
at his post,
in a little hat, cockeyed as himself,
with a deaf-mute dog. The urgent sun-fire
calls me from the windows of La Messuguière tower.
                    Once more turn toward Cabris:
an acropolis in the gold of tiles.
Because the sun bids us farewell in gold
before it departs. Then
in chalky violet
before the night extinguishes it.
Before the night extinguishes us
little fires of human bustle will flare up below.
How good it is to be at home, at last, facing silence.
Purify yourself with censers of sulphur, wool, fire,
fir twigs, in sacral silks
meditate by a candle, with Seneca. *Aetas
serenitatis;* beyond the pass of old age
there is peace. Words, words. Seneca fell from your hand long ago.
You dream, old fogy, you daydream, daydrumdream. . . .

IX

It is the nature of the highest objective art to be clean. The Muses are maidens.
                    —A. LANG, *Homer and Anthropology*

So beautiful the lungs
are breathless. The hand remembers:
I was a wing.
Blue. The peaks in ruddy
gold. Women of that land—
small olives. On a spacious saucer
wisps of smoke, houses, pastures, roads.
Interlacing of roads, o holy diligence
of man. How hot it is! The miracle
of shade returns. A shepherd, sheep, a dog, a ram
all in gilded bells. Olive trees
in twisted benevolence. A cypress—their lone shepherd. A village

on a Cabris cliff, protected
by its tiled roofs. And a church, its cypress and shepherd.
Young day, young times, young world.
Birds listen, intently silent. Only a rooster crowing
from below in the hamlet of Spéracèdes. How
hot it is. It's bitter to die on foreign soil.
It's sweet to live in France.

    X

For whom is the garden planted?
Who is happy there?
No eyes to be my haven.
How can the heart sustain dying?
Something creeps behind me.
Fear falls away.
What fell in the abyss?
Let the scream resound.
A hand looms above.
A smile hangs suspended.
Don't look at me, my wife.
Son, let my hand go.

    XI

TO MY WIFE
ON OUR THIRTY-FIFTH WEDDING ANNIVERSARY

Enmeshed in the frenzies of praying mantises.
Of Nature's creations, what is more sublime
than a family? Wife, husband, child—
the golden division of the species, the lesser becomes the greater,
and so the tribe renews itself in the festoons of time.
              O, mountain stream
              Basalt beneath
              Bedrock of flight
              Pendulum-home
              Vise of the heart

Lily of the soul
Contralto of quiet
And faithful shroud.
Violet—sorrow,
In winter flakes,
O, you warm earth
Of peaks and valleys!
In sickness and in health
Siamese sister
My Bride.

La Messuguière, January–April 1962

DREAMS FROM THE SHORE OF THE MEDITERRANEAN

"O God! I could be bounded in a nutshell, and count myself a king of infinite space, were it not that I have bad dreams."
—HAMLET II, *ii*

*"The Lord constantly punished us and constantly terrified us
With fires, the black death, the witch of hunger,
With eyes of unknown stars, horrible dreams
And princes mad at our freedom."*
—SLOWACKI, *Prince Michael of Tver*

1.

Using both hands, my senses in rapt attention, gently,
                      you see, Doctor,
I always carried before me, like a lantern, a cage
                 made of tender reeds
and a butterfly whose name I don't know circled in it.
Not so much white as woven of light, only the ribbing
was thick, not transparent. I say "lantern" for indeed it
       illuminated
the road before me. Yes, it was night, but made radiant dawn
by the butterfly. And the road led through oily tidelands, true,
                  shallow, but there your leg sinks and sloshes.
Their colors brought to mind pigeons' throats when
                after my nightly rounds
of the city, I returned to my warm home at daybreak,
              a sturdy Ahasuerus
chased by a judgment never proclaimed but almost always
                an inkling. And you know,
I was so deep in thought, so bewildered by the
              excess of forebodings,
that my butterfly broke away from me. With the
              strength of an eagle.
Speeding at first like a stone, not down—up. Then moving
              to the west. But since I
pursued my opposing way, it suddenly turned and

                    again started to circle
near me, rotating faster, much more angrily,
oh, it even crowed once or twice, though till now had
                    been mortally silent.
This, Doctor, was repeated exactly three times. In vain, at home
my mother waited for me, under her starched sheet; I had to fulfill
the ancient duty of a son. So my butterfly, no more butterfly,
—now a bird, gave up on me with a wave of its broad wing
and seemed to be not angry, not at all, just in despair. About me.
And flew off, for ever, so now, Doctor,
must I forever do without the lantern? And what does
                    that dream mean, Doctor?
But please, this time, no sex. That's not what I need:
                    what I need is breath
nourishing, for my lungs, a light for my heart,
                    earthly food for my eyes.
For it's dark, the road leads through suffocating marshes,
                    and I am left without lantern, without wings,
without the cage, and I really don't know what to
                    do with my freedom
when I no longer have my butterfly.

2.

I spent the early years of my youth
in the belly of a fish. From the old species
Balistes capricus. I was not quite
thirteen, when it spat me out. Indeed, in a fine parabola.
What a trip!
                    I still haven't come to my senses
after the shock of birth. It seemed the trajectory
would never reach its goal!
I scared gulls, oh, not those sweet ones, forever sweet to us
our native swallows. My left leg caught on a chimney
tall and leaning unnaturally—ship after ship,
battleships, schooners. From dazzling upper decks
I was observed through binoculars. Radiantly naked
ladies in topsail hairdos, laden with jewels,
induced in me a state of shame. The more so since I myself

was, after all, naked. *Passons.* So, it's a seaport. Tyre? Sidon? Perhaps
Syracuse? Yet, uncertain, I ask
its name. How they started shouting! Waving their arms!
Undoing spells! (In contortions and secretly, I know this,
I practiced it myself.) How they were scat-ter-ing! So where am I,
for heaven's sake? Those heavy tits, those
puppet faces, those colored wigs exposed behind windowpanes
to the glare? Not one of them winks, though their eyes incessantly
turn. Pretty, those eyes, one green, the other hazel. And
                                              before her, and her, and her
a stein. Or else *un bock.* As on rue Blondel, for two francs.
Arrogant Bruno caught a glass through the windowpane,
tilts his horselike head, sips, puts it aside,
"Good beah," smacks his lips, falls, he will die in labor-camp
agony, in the distant, oh, how distant North. Poor
                                                woodcutter. Let's recite
a quick prayer for him. A gang of woodcutters returns
                            from work. "A bell rings for prayers . . ."
they sing. I am tired of all this. Where is my fish?
                                     Back there, right now!
I ask. All of you are deaf and dumb in this city.
                        In the damned city. In this city
you are damned. In a sentenced city. Forever. "Order a
                                   procession," I say imperiously
to the mayor. "Let them solemnly circle the walls,
                                 purify with incense
the unclean gates, as it is Februarius, the month of expiation."
Deaf as a post, he stands, breast to pointed breasts, with his naked,
jewel-laden wench. Everybody here with his naked wench.
                            Only I'm alone. Alone
I loiter in these tortuous, damned little streets.
                                And everything began
so promisingly: Swallows in flight, *Kinder an*
                                Reinheit! So I sit down,
spent, in a gutter. This is Sidon. Vicolo d'Amor
                                Perfetto. Luminous,
white skeletons of ships, of sailboats, all the purchasable colors
from postcards. Of a Sentenced city.
                        So I squat under the bougainvillea, the
                            one from the quarries

where naked Artemises in topsail hairdos, laden with jewels,
shot at us with golden bows, looking at our agony
                              from above. At agony—
always from above. When not seen from above, what is agony?
                              One cloud curiously white
floats away.

3.

Tue-les, howls the mob. *Ausrotten,*
screeches a parrot in a white jabot;
an English-tailored suit; grayish
bangs; she is slender, bony and chic;
her eye—a flaring sapphire against gray flannel.
Tue-les—howls the mob. How hard it is
to move my legs. Though conversations of one's
                              countrymen are sweet,
let us look up their sleeves. *Ausrotten,* screeches
a lady with a parrot's head, she slipped into
the crowd undulating on the sidewalks, but in the empty
middle of the roadway—it's me, only me, a little
Jew, a poor Algerian—me again, me,
until it's hard to bear. She: *Ausrotten.* The others
                              are already hoarse.
A warm hand on my forehead: "Wake up." Nothing equals
a loving hand on your forehead. But still so much road
before me. Now a flower with the face of a bestial child.
Ausrotten! And birds are silent. And the Hunter
listens with a steel gun barrel—a phallic symbol? By the way,
is it possible to do one's own psychoanalysis while sleeping?
Once I succeeded. . . . In the "Siberia" of the Warsaw neurology
clinic, where the epileptic Y*** kept jumping up
and throwing his arm wildly. *Tue-les,* they howled then
outside the window. Old M***'s death rattle came from above his
hanging jaw, a withered Ramses, he will die in the morning
under the loudspeaker which will splutter sweet
                              cream of wheat for the hog
and a plump wench will scratch her unsleepy behind
          bandaging with her other hand that unruly

jaw. But you were nearby! Kill, kill, rattled
                                      the mob outside the window.
            And birds are silent. And in the mountains
the Hunter. But you are with me, now nothing can
                                      happen to us. Let's go.
How difficult it is to lift my foot. *Ausrotten,* screeches
                                      the parrot in the jabot.
Let's go on. How easy it is
to descend uphill.

    4.

TO MY SISTERS SEDA AND CESIA

At the Greek's, behind the shop window, the sea—sponges,
    lobsters—
the top sky high. On display, cakes
with pointed bellies, tawny, olive, coral-red.
Behind the shop window my three sisters walk, one after the
    other.
How far will they get?—I fall into meditation. Thus, behind
                                    the shop window, the sea.
We dropped in at the Greek's for a moment. But
            the sea, obnoxious sea, the top sky-high,
its layers innumerable. And they are so
wavy. Cakes, yes: 1, $\sqrt{-7}$, alef°,: o.
I am cheating, I know. Whereas the Greek makes
                          change honestly: three kopecks—
coppers, I feel their taste in my fingertips—only this was missing
to get dragged by the scruff to my childhood's first dreams!
So I dream. I dream *ergo* I sleep. All the better.
                              I dream in Eastman—
Color. What did Askanas call this? The second system—but of
                              what? I don't remember.
I prattle and my three sisters make their feet sore.
                        The fourth one,
an adolescent mimosa, waits downstairs, by
                          the door. Let Ola lead me
out of the sea. Let us sail away. On little sleighs.

                              In the park, of Ujazdów,
I will look at the swans, sob. My hair flying
from my skull—where I have as a permanent resident
                              a centenarian lobster,
my little contemporary, striped with sapphire and minium—
will surface, a silver medusa, alone and without me.

   5.

TO PROF. DR. ZDZISLAW ASKANAS

The snow on my eyes has melted, bony fingers on my neck
have turned into a necklace. Then You, dear, came running
drawn to a passerby's shout behind the window. What can
       he know,
a passerby on this earth of the well-settled? I remember,
a braggart stag, proud of his necklace,
a changing rainbow in sunny dew,
walked through Walicόw, and in a window open to summer
fragrance, to an array of lilacs and of chestnut trees in bloom
a boy was sitting. He wore a skullcap,
his black eyes stared nowhere. I remember,
the stag mocked, he said something so mocking
that the child withdrew into the room,
                              offended.
Inside there was a bed, on it a form
absolutely horizontal (as somewhere in Rembrandt).
That stag, what did he know? He was a passerby on this earth
of the settled. Oh, he knew enough, when he was slowly walking
home. What could be done? He wept. The necklace
chokes my throat. Break it, let the bone beads
scatter. Years, places, dark
attachments, they also scatter.
Then the Hunter arrives, drawn by a shout,
and weighs on his hand all your poor treasures,
as if he wanted to return them to you. But he only looks
and weighs, one after the other, and drops one
              after the other in the dust of the street.
The snow on your eyes already melted, you may wake up.

6.

When I meet an elephant, I shall ask him for his doctor's
 address.
I could also ask my neighbor, a palm tree, it's
                        thick-skinned enough,
but I know: it won't even mutter back, it slights me.
This makes me so uneasy! Thin-skinned, I haven't
                        gone out of the house
for ages, though—ah! I am lured
by Les Grands Boulevards. Most of all on Sunday,
in the late afternoon, in the heat of summer,
                        when even the tourists
have taken shelter in their nests by the sea. I simply love the mobs
swarming out of their tenements. Young mothers with
                        sleepy kids, chic salesmen,
stately married couples and ethereal girls from brainless
streets, colorful dayflies. Neon lights from movie houses
caress them all with the luster of brief happiness.
Which is refused to me. I've locked myself in a narrow
cage at my hotel and so days and years pass me by.
                        No, a hundred times no,
I don't want them looking through my skin at my shame:
those tangles, veinlets, those coils, nervures, those textures—
a nonfigurative painting in which every gaper
will see what suits him: one—flotillas dragging nets, another—
nightmares with snouts telescoped into dogs', frogs' paws.
                        Somebody else—
a dump where a scavenger, once the pearl of bordellos,
rakes out her poor treasures with a stick. Or, for a change—
streams, Euphratean tributaries, five-branched rivers
                        veining black earth, or—
a lode of gneiss, marbled with lime, yellow clay, carnelian.
And, somebody very cruel—a work of a mad
                        craftsman, a mute organ
which no one has ever played and on which nothing
                        will ever be played.

7.

TO ANDRÉ AND FRANÇOISE

L'immense baleine se nourrit de minuscules
Copepodes et Schizopodes.
—H. DECUGIS, *Le Vieillissement du monde vivant*

The night watchman walked into the well-heated house, ringing
his keys, and sat down on the King's bed. They play cards.
Early morning. Before the window a red vine streams down
curtainlike, incessantly, and fences us from
savage passersby in skins: they are Mongols, they shoot
their matchlock muskets at little birds which this night inhabited
the King's dreams. The most wicked of the King's daughters,
now an Amazon, gambols under the surface of ponds and her two
greyhounds chase a carp. In its old eyes,
thanks to a foolish arrangement of Nature, is reflected
the eidolon of the King, when he plays cards with the watchman,
his most faithful chamberlain. With him every night,
after he wakes up, before he falls asleep again, the King strolls
back and forth, back and forth, in front of his palace
which trembles like jelly, though the structure
is substantial. What do they talk about? What do they gamble for?
Me, no doubt. Perhaps. Though after all I am
less than a snail and a tenant of His Majesty's grass
only by His favor. Sometimes they invite me in
for a meal, i.e., a feast. One crunches a nice goose in a sauce
of sour beets, stuffed with snails from the same royal garden.
Savage passersby shoot muskets, blow twisted horns,
which does not disturb at all the festive eclogues at our table.
Beyond a wine-colored curtain the light of a tallow candle,
the only one here: thrifty housekeeping and
                                       family warmth are provided,
oh yes. Right now passersby, a band, girls from Les Halles
will enter. I will slip down along the drooping tablecloth
under the table where cards are scattered. There I shall wait out
December, drunkards' hiccups, a flight, with a tremolo of fifes,
to the moon, lack of cash, manifestations of the people
and the mistral which constantly drones in this region.

In my region, not at all. And the trees are different, more sturdy,
in other words: more humane. And they cast a denser shade,
allowing the moss to spread softly under the noiseless steps
of the Hunter. While in their crowns one can hide
and be secure. Though to be sure, here under the table
the dogs will do me no harm either. They yawn.
That's fine.

    8.

FOR CZESLAW MILOSZ

They who support my arm, will they be stopped by the aroma
of vineyards? A huge bell of air—will they hear in their lungs
its silver sound? Now my lungs alone feel the young spring,
they alone sate themselves with the young rustling of the
                                day over the stream
of herbs and seas. But they, their grasp never
                                slackens and their gaze
is stony. An imaginable deer darts before us, hides in a thicket,
spots flash by in the grass, now stands in sunlight
                                by a water hole
and looks at the bony shells of its horns bathed
in the golden flecks of the stream. But you must move on.
           Forward or backward—I don't know.
They who lead us by the arm and have a stony gaze.
                          Yet they too should see
these stones all around! Should slacken their grip, should be swayed
by the rocks' expression: of surprise? adoration? menace?
These gestures of sacrificers, of the sacrificed, of
                          orantes! Here a knight,
weary into death, who returned from a long war, rested his head
against the rooftree of his house long since turned to stone, where
   moss
dwells and desolation and a flighty lizard; where the locust, slim
   dancer,
has sped to the hunt from a heavy cocoon, having
                        stuck it with saliva
onto calcite, ages would pass and not unglue it, a sturdy buck

would gobble the young and the gnawed nest
                              endures. Like the ruins
of a City. They who lead by the arm are angels.
                         Surely angels. Oh, not the kind
that dive from above. Neither the breath, so pure,
                    of those from above
nor the silver tone of their trumpets will trouble them who
     guide me.
They are messengers, only messengers, nothing more, their route
traced from the beginning of time. Let's go on. Let's trample
moss, lizards, let's blister our feet on the pumice of the road
through the petrified sands of deserts, let's mark
                         with a bloody zigzag
a trail for others. Let him who wants to,
flap his wing, it's powerless, but he gives the soul élan.
Let's pass Artemises by the stream, laundresses,
                    maybe, Greek, or Jewish.
The clatter of paddles animates Nature. It lauds
                    Her, daughter of Dione.
Here everything lauds the daughter of Dione. Let
                    me come near the well,
let me look into the eyes of Rachel. But they who guide me
will not swerve from the road. And I, too, keep in mind
the adventure of a man who preceded me. He did
                         not turn into salt but—
oh, the heart's eternal sorrow!
          Owls' eyes in the alders
                         we pass. And the eyes
of a peacock's tail. Peacocks ceased screeching
                    their strangled complaint.
For everything fell silent at once out of pity:
                    looking on your *disgrace.*
Yes, since you are dragged, towed, by your hair, your legs.
The eyes, all the eyes are averted and now only silence
lauds the daughter of Dione. Who eternally rises from the seas,
radiant. High is such praise. But you do not hear
that graceful silence. To the brim of memory
                    you are full of voices.
Voices from the house, voices from the garden, voices
                         from the forest, voices

from above you—they are gone and yet remain
                                      and will not go away
even when the abortive human species disappears;
                            they will enter into
swallows, mosses, insects, stones, nothingness
                                   if necessary. Into silence
which is the voice of the voice primeval.
        They, angels, who drag you, stone
is not in their eyes, their eyes in truth are tender and human,
but their eyes see only stone.
        Their blood does not trace their route
and their eyes are not stone, not at all, they are unfathomable,
the same and changing, tender human eyes. But they
            see only one thing: the stone of your heart.
Besides, everything lauds the daughter of Dione who eternally
emerges from the seas, radiant, her hair luxuriously curled.
But your ears are tightly sealed with beeswax.
                              Sealed against silence.
Yet something penetrates them: the distant creaking
                              of a peasant cart.
And peasant chatter echoing from the forest,
those voices untaught, not taught by Nature—
as even minerals, even a mole, even blades of grass are—
but not our churlish, dear tender peasant
voices:
        That's my gravediggers singing.

La Messuguière and Cabris, February–March 1962

A FEW AUTHOR'S NOTES

SONGS OF A WANDERER

Song II

into the stone world: Préalpes de Grasse. Hard limestone from the early Jurassic age; later stratifications of chalk, gypsum, sand; marine deposits from the Pliocene age. Here and there the wavy profile of many formations is exposed. Landslides of flint, porous blocks of volcanic lava, metamorphic rocks, gneiss veined with black mica; below, nummolite stratifications, soft sandstone. The bas-relief of the terrain is boldly variegated in a state of *becoming,* of incompleteness visible to the naked eye. The folds of the mountains, overlapping, eroded by labyrinthine ravines and gorges of the streams Siagne and Loup, encircle large plateaus and plains with their rings open to the sea. Covered by a mass of luxuriant greenery right up to the tall summits of the cliffs; of trees, the olive and low evergreen cork oaks and many varieties of acacias predominate; here and there, clumps of stone pine, no lack of poplars, alders, figs and cypress trees; myrtles, hard, steel-green agaves; a countless abundance of shrubs and herbs—everything on that ungrateful soil, subject to chemical and physical erosion, fertilized by the toil of so many generations. The eagle's nests of old villages—small fortified towns. The air so clear that on calm mornings the shores of Corsica, about two hundred kilometers away, become visible and the scale of light values surpasses every painter's palette.

On the other hand, beyond the nearest pass is another world: the cupola-like profile of the Trias, bare mountains with snow on the ridges of their peaks, here and there the olive-drab smudges of lichens and dwarf mountain pine, the barren Provence. Amphitheaters of volcanic rock, also perhaps of archaic megaliths—with forms so chimerical they could serve as the scenery for a *Walpurgisnacht.* There—the turbulent, multiform bulk of the becoming world, here—the monotonous agony of space.

Song IV

by the Vengeful Hand (Jehovah's): A not sufficiently exact translation of *"Beyod hazoko,"* containing the idea of might and violence, but certainly of vengeance as well.

Grasse: An old, picturesque town eighteen kilometers from the sea. At present its chief industry is perfumes.

In lieblicher Bläue . . .: A poem by Friedrich Hölderlin from his late period (vol. VI, Propyläen-Verlag), beginning with these words.

in a dark hat: Very old women sometimes seem the sole inhabitants of Cabris (those younger and the men work in Grasse): they never show themselves outside the house except when wearing a hat; straw, flat, with a wide brim, dark gray or gray-brown patined by rain and time—to a stranger it makes an impression like a uniform for those preparing for death.

Song V

A small scene from life, pedantically realistic with the interpolation of an inner monologue by the author. Only the names have been changed.

magi descended: In the last few years the ancient procession of the Three Kings in medieval Provençal costumes has been resumed here.

Diana Hecate Luna: The triple incarnation of Artemis. N.B. The reminiscence from *Delie* (XIII: "Like Hecate you make me err") by Maurice Scève, a great poet of the sixteenth century. To distinguish her (or not) from the three-headed Hecate-Persephone of Hades.

from the valleys of Fergana: Molotovobad, in Uzbekistan, where the author found himself in the spring of 1942. The configuration of mountainous terrain, the physiognomy of the flora (in the sense used by W. von Humboldt, *Ansichten der Natur*), its general synoptic looks, trees in pathetic gesticulations, the dramatic "happenings" of the landscape, the clarity of the air, the multigrade intensity of the light—all that, strange thing, brings to mind the place in Provence in which the present verses were written.

Song VI

Cf. the speech of A. Shelepin, the chief of the security police of the USSR, at the XXII Congress. Cit. *Cahiers du Communisme*, No. 12, 1961, p. 291: "Staline écrivit sur cette lettre (of the imprisoned general Jakir): 'scélérat et prostitue,' Voroshilov ajouta: 'définition parfaîtement exacte.' . . . Kaganovitsch écrivit encore: 'Au traître, à la crapule et (suit un mot obscène) un seul chatîment: la mort.'"

Song VII

Saint Dionysius: The pseudo-Areopagite, identified by church tradition with the martyr and first bishop of Paris (Lutetia), who is depicted with his own cut-off head in his hand. According to his theological treatise *De divinis nominibus*, evil is only the tendency of finite things to non-being; speaking metaphorically: "a zero, itself not existing, as a multiplier of any being gives zero." Since Being is indestructible, even the devil therefore cannot be immanently evil, for he would cease to be. In a word, evil is non-being (non-ens), but the temporal evil which we endure—our own sufferings, those inflicted by others, illnesses—exists in our finite world exclusively in so far as it is good.

Song VIII

I swear obscenely, play backgammon: Cf. Machiavelli's letter to Francesco Vettori: "Twilight falls, I return home from the tavern, I throw off my filthy rags, dress myself in regally sacral silks, to hold intercourse with the ancients in the still of the library."

Centauresses defending the Throne: Cf. my book *Me from One Side and Me from the Other Side of My Pug-Iron Stove* (Warsaw, 1920).

La Messuguière: Estate near Cabris, a foundation for French intellectuals established by Andrée Vienot, where these verses were written.

of sulphur, wool: A Roman ritual of purification and expiation *(februatio)*.

Song XI

the golden division: The whole is to the greater part as it is to the smaller: $\frac{a+b}{a} = \frac{a}{b}$.

From antiquity it ranks as the most harmonious arrangement, used with pleasure in architecture, in art and also in crystals, in the morphology of plants and even of numerous sea creatures, and in the form of the human body. (Luca Pacioli, in the treatise *De divina proportione*, 1509, calls it divine. Hambridge in *Dynamic Symmetry* demonstrates that it makes possible the creation of further divisions with the preservation of an identical morphological theme. N.B. This information is taken from the work of M. C. Ghyka, *La Proportion dans les arts plastiques*, in *L'Encyclopédie française*, vol. XVI.)

DREAMS FROM THE SHORE OF THE MEDITERRANEAN

Second Dream

Balistes capricus: A fish from the family *Balistidae*. I repeat in a free paraphrase what de Lacépède has written about it (*Histoire naturelle*, vol. II, Paris, 1836): In the cruel world of fish and sea monsters, the *Balistidae* are distinguished by a philosophic gentleness. They are armored, indeed they know how to defend themselves, but they themselves do not attack, their food is not other fish: they do not sow terror, nor are they subject to it. Nature has granted them a rare charm, the gift of the light and the warmth of hot seas, colors pleasing to the eye and properly contrasted. The Mediterranean variety of *Balistes capricus* is light violet, has the reflexes of a pigeon's throat, incrustations of azure and aquamarine, vermilion fins; its large eyes encircled in bright yellow are "like sapphires in a golden setting." The English call their less conspicuous variety "old wife." Their bellies are particularly extendable, which makes it easy for them to fill with air, and consequently gives them mobility and manoeuvrability in diving. Their flesh is poisonous.

Bruno: Bruno Jasieński in Paris in 1926.

"The bell rings for prayers, Mother calls for supper, time to go home now, they're calling us home now": From the song "Though the Storm Roars Around Us," sung by Poles in prisons and in remote Soviet labor camps.

Kinder an Reinheit: From Hölderlin's poem *"In lieblicher Bläue . . . ."*

Vicolo d'Amor Perfetto: A filthy alley in Genoa with very old prostitutes.

the bougainvillea, the one from the quarries: A real one, beautifully developed, at the exit of the deep quarries (Latomia del Paradiso) in Syracuse. In the fifth century B.C., the Athenian youth taken into slavery perished there beneath a scorching sun (cf. Thucydides, *The Pelopponesian War*). This was certainly the first extermination camp in history. Now—it is a paradise of birds and vegetation.

Third Dream

in the "Siberia": Thus the patients reviled the neurology ward at the Infant Jesus Hospital in Warsaw, where the author was a patient in the beginning of 1953.

under the loudspeaker: At that time, in hospital wards loudspeakers were obligatory from morning until ten in the evening.

Fourth Dream

At the Greek's: Before 1914, a bakery popular in Warsaw, owned by Greeks who also engaged in peddling sponges.

Fifth Dream

somewhere in Rembrandt: In the National Museum in Brussels a painting by Rembrandt depicting a dead woman.

Eighth Dream

the rocks' expression: A stone amphitheater with fantastic shapes, on the road to St. Vallier, possibly megaliths of a very ancient ritual site.
daughter of Dione: Aphrodite.
everything lauds: From the Orphic hymns.
the adventure of a man: Orpheus, who could accompany Eurydice from Hades on the condition—which wasn't fulfilled—that he did not look her in the eye.

III

ODE II

TO JAN LEBENSTEIN

And what should I look back at in a desert
diaspora of your cities: while he clutched me by
the nape and won't let me go and forces me to an
asthmatic trot there where my eyes no more can tear themselves
away from the implacable Eye, ever.

Where will I find signs of our tribal encampments,
where do we have our wells, our roads and crossroads,
our gates and cities, our oracles, pillories?

What remained of Ur, Babylon, Nineveh?

Sands have buried their wild splendor, gods
have decomposed in mortuaries of museums,
and their inhabitants, long ago turned to dust,
vibrate in the sand, forever.

Only the embittered longing of my heart remains,
and in the visible world of galuth—O shame!—
an unbroken line: in the ill-smelling alleys
of your rues de Beausire flocks of harlots
reproduce in every generation, they alone—O shame!—
old civilizations;
only here the unaging face of the Babylonian whore,
gestures of priestesses of the Lady of Biblos,
at the street corners a biblical prostitute—and, had
a Median warrior hot from battle with his quiver
and arrows stood before her, she would have led him
to a hotel as she does a neighboring shopkeeper.

So on that desert of galuth where I languish away,
day after day, I am stuck
—O shame!—
in a stinking joint, among pimps and sluts,

and in their loathsome company
I visualize myself in my city, Nineveh,
at the time of my prophet,
Jonah.

ODE III

TO ALBERT VALLETTE

With my skin I experienced a Creation full of gifts, of friendly surfaces, of light's smiles, of smells and sounds, all that was pleasing to the senses. With my skin I experienced Creation from the first morning till late evening, till the nightfall, while it was bringing testimony to itself: "It is good";

with my skin I approached you, my friends, with my skin when it was the first geography of brotherhood, when it was an algorithm, the first, of tenderness;

with my skin I tasted every earthly thing, sunrises and sunsets, the infinity of moments between them, the Eleatic space and the force or the burden of minutes as heavy as mother's breasts, hills and lowlands, and every quarter of the globe and everything angelic suddenly encountered;

renouncing disputes, with my skin I questioned my God. And I questioned the snake. Also created Nature and everything which is of it.

With my skin I measured uncountable dimensions of time-space, with it I fathomed the flights of youth and the downfalls of the age of defeats.

To be in the skin, in everyone, in every skin of every one, in yellow, white, black, red, and the one stripped of meat;

let us begin with skin—I called—o reformers! or else: O mortals!—I called—in a holy alliance enjoined upon us, of "I" and "you";

thus nothing that is from the skin was alien to me, nothing that comes from its perishable matter exposed to destruction, ruined by time and violence, nothing that is from its indestructible energy. From the skin which is pure in spite of all its erosions and shames.

And so I was carrying lightly in myself the Asias of skin, the continents of skin, always on the run, always in dance, a swift-legged knight of Hermes, of Shiva and of Eros, also of Eros with his torch inverted.

I used to escape into the skin when Baseness and Crime stopped me on the road, along with the retinue of that hideous pair, Death-done-to-others; also, when suddenly I would confront on the road the sublime terror of existence.

With my skin I was your constant companion in the stench of prisons and hospitals, my skin responding, vibrating, echoing to the sufferings of your skins.

And with my skin I wallowed in the shallow bays of the cities, in the jungles of *natura naturata* and on the sweet greens of *natura naturans*.

In the valleys of the skin I was finding seclusion and shade and I washed it with live water from a fountain to which only the deer would come to drink.

In the skin, to put it briefly, was my joy. And my glory at the moments when my sullen brain fed me with cyanide, ineffectively;

when I, in my pride, promised to myself to thrust out wisdom from the prison cell of the skull and to spread it all over the infinite, though so finite, expanse of the skin, *gaia scienza;*

when I, a fool, tried to make my speech consubstantial with my skin so that it says nothing beyond "tiu-tiu-tiu-tiam-tiam-tiam."

Now, when I am tightly sewn in my skin, imprisoned in my skin, it, the skin, is a great misfortune to me, a great, great misfortune, even though my brain, stultified by old age, intones, and how, hey! a hosanna of coexisting in the Lord, alleluia!

In the skin is my misfortune, a great, great misfortune, in the skin grilled, lacerated, ploughed every day anew with fiery pain, since the first dawn through the unending expanse of empty moments till the latest evening, also in the hideous spells of awakenings terrifying as knife revelations.

It is true, Hell has been promised to me long ago, but is not the promise being fulfilled too early? I submit this to your consideration, o distinguished guardians of balances—and against the accepted rules?

And of no use to me was my seeing you through, o Ploughman, and through the fierceness of your labor in man, that image and likeness of God, as we have been called once, to hearten us? out of mercy? perhaps out of mockery?

Therefore I bequeath to you, my brethren, my skin, naked skin, for what else do I have? with a humble prayer, to tan it for the binding of this collection of stanzas;

they, ugly-beautiful, good-evil as they are, are from both that ecstatic skin and this ploughed, grilled, lacerated skin of a sacrificial beast that is dying without profit for a long, long, long time, before a butcher's dull knife glints in its eyes.

A TURTLE FROM OXFORD

TO K. JELENSKI

*And when the queen of Sheba heard of
the fame of Solomon concerning the name
of the Lord, she came to prove him with
hard questions.*
— I KINGS 10

On the eastern sidewalk of Magdalen College a small
turtle reflected a long time before he answered
my question, he moved his jaws like a meccano: "That,
even I cannot remember: I am hardly
two hundred and ninety-three. But in our family
a record has been preserved how our ancestor, of blessed memory,
assisted at the lovemaking of the queen of Sheba with
                                        your great-grandfather.
As to the riddles she presumably asked him to solve, our tradition
is silent. What is known: it occurred in a wine-colored chamber
where, instead of lamps, gold was shining, from Tyre, no doubt.
My ancestor was not a learned turtle, but a respectable one,
to be sure. . . ."

With short steps we shuffled after him, I, my beautiful
wife and Adriana, our charming guide.
We listened to the turtle solemnly. When he lost his breath
my wife with a kind stroke of her finger
animated his little snout. After all, that's why I wander!
In strange lands! In my old age!
I write, that is to say, my autobiography and gather data
for the genealogy of our ancient stock. An English duke
in a waterfront dive in Naples brought the turtle to my attention,
in return for a bowl of spaghetti and a glass
of wine ("My great-great-grandfather, an admiral,
took that turtle to Oxford all the way from Abyssinia").
Thus all three of us listened to the turtle with the solemnity due
to a dignified university person. But now

the pause was irritatingly long, when all of a sudden,
from behind an island, young laughter was heard
and a boat passed, carrying a couple away.
Neither of them graceful. But my wife was delighted
to hear laughter of lovers. There is no need to add
that, tiptoeing after the turtle and straining to hear
what he might deign to tell us, we were bent so low
that one might say we were on all fours.
Were they laughing at this? At their love?
At love in general? It does not matter.
                              "So, hardly had
he turned over on his back when he asked: 'And *now*
tell me, baby, what do they think of me in your country?'
The queen, still in ecstasies: 'That you love wisdom,'
she faltered, 'and women.' 'Wisdom?' he replied, 'I don't deny.
But women? Hardly. I love femininity.'"

Again there was a pause. This time not laughter but crying
and that of an infant, indeed, more bizarre here
than, for instance, a drunkard's railing in a cathedral.

                    "And he was right,"
the turtle added at last. "He was wrong!" exclaimed
charming Adriana, blushing all over. She never interrupted
her elders, since she was well-bred. "He was right,"
the turtle repeated, as though he had not heard. "A great lord
should love only universals: grassiness, not grass,
not humans, humanity, and arsiness, not . . ."
                              Whether he finished or not
I don't know, for Adriana again interjected, it is true, somewhat
abashed: "He who never loved someone, doesn't know love
at all." The turtle fell silent, for good; now he had taken
offense: nobody here had dared to contradict him.
We had no flies or anything else to smooth over the incident.
But my wife, who has a way with animals
and children, gently massaged his jowls.
So he spoke again, this time even garrulously:

"When King Solomon rolled off the queen for the third time,
he asked: 'Now, what counsel do your people ask for?

What do they want from me?' 'A toenail,' answered
the queen of Sheba, 'from the little toe of your foot.'
'I'll give it to them,' agreed the king, and himself
handed her a pair of nail scissors. She pulled out a golden cup
artfully engraved by the hand of Hiram-Abi,
which the king after their first intercourse had presented to her.
It had a tight-fitting lid, on it was carved the grim face of
    Ashtoreth.
A short cry, blood spurted into the cup, the lid clicks shut. . . .
What happened next, our ancestor did not relate.
Perhaps the whole thing so tired him, the strain upon his eyes,
upon his attention, that he suddenly fell asleep.
He was not learned. Who, after all, in those times,
was learned?"
        "But what happened to the cup?
The cup?" I asked hollowly. For just then
a thought disturbed me, that perhaps
if I drink the blood of my ancestor,
youth, eternal, wisdom, forever, will be restored to me!

        "Oh yes," the turtle replied impassively,
"we know. The ship carrying the queen back, sank. Thirteen
centuries later Senegalese sailors extracted the cup
from the belly of a whale, in the Indian Ocean." "Undamaged?"
"Undamaged." Again a pause. "From Abyssinia, an Italian airman
stole it together with the treasure of the King of Kings
not long ago. . . . His plane fell into Etna."
"Into Etna!" I cried in falsetto, I straightened up
as well as I could and I raised my arms into the air,
frightening by this motion two male cardinals
that were fighting a knightly battle
on the grass, plucking at each other's beautiful scarlet crests.
"And yet Etna threw back the cup,"
unexpectedly screeched the turtle. "Like a
        sandal?" "Of Empedocles,"
he asserted with vivid satisfaction. Again silence. The crying
of the infant had long subsided. And the laugh of the lovers.
And the hissing of the birds. I could not stand this stillness.
"Where is the blood of my ancestor?" I shouted, full of hope.
        "Blood, blood, blood,"

he grated angrily. Adriana got up: "I wanted, master,
to sit at your feet and imbibe the words of wisdom from your
lips. And now . . ." She sobbed, poor, dear Adriana. "Blood,
of blood, with blood," repeated the turtle, obviously unable to stop.
"You gulped the blood of my cousins, is not that enough? Seizing
them in whole fistfuls in the bulrushes by the river Ili, crushing and
smashing them with a rolling pin, on the rough table in the kitchen
of the Prokombinat where you helped the dirty woman cook to
steal food. The blood of my brothers splashed into your eyes,
bespattered your face, your rags, you waded in their blood, still you
didn't have enough. You have never had enough. Not
                                        enough. Not enough. Not
enough . . ."

I was afraid that he would have a stroke, he was choking.
Ashamed, we fled across the lawns and for a long time
the gargoyles of Magdalen pursued us with their howling laughter.

Oxford, July 1962

TAKING A WALK

Temeh, Cain's wife, and Tirzah, Abel's widow,
were taking a walk along the edge of Eden, this side of the
    barbed-wire wall.
From the towers winged soldiers shouted warnings, gaily,
roguishly: Watch out! A million macrovolts! No doubt they
    exaggerated.
Thistles hardly breed here. Nearby, in the Mountains, dwarf
    pines.
Earth is like dry rot. A hundred days without rain. But
in one corner a colony of burdocks prospers,
also a settlement of toads. A little spring trickles there
from the underground waters of the river Pishon. In which river,
as is known from the Holy Writ (Genesis 2, 11), gold is
for the picking. And pure as gold. Young sons of Cain
toil on, extracting it, under guard, from dawn till night.
Not hard work. And profitable. And the air is brisk,
very healthful.
Rats would sneak to that spring from Eden,
also moles. For a change of climate? Of mood?

Temeh and Tirzah have so much to tell each other!
About that row.
And who started it? They were brothers, after all.
It's easy to say: a row. For one—an eternal spout of tears!
A mystery of widowhood. To the other—the subject of incessant
adoration for her husband, ox-necked laborer.
While Temeh jabbers about muscles (and saliva flicks from the
    corners of her mouth)
Tirzah thinks: ". . . a jerk . . . but mine was tender-skinned.
A nimble-legged hunter. Swifter than any deer. And the string of
    his bow
sounded like a golden string of a lute. On which lute the mother Eve
thrums in the brown of dusk, in the twilight, when she yearns after
the snake, when he was young and handsome, after the lost, ha,

happiness; and the stupid old fool (he suspects nothing)
> asks her to thrum
>> and thrum
—he finds in this thrumming his dream, the first, when the
> Master Surgeon
opened his side, took out a rib, anachronistic and painful,
and after coating it nicely in mellow flesh, split it somewhat at the
> bottom,
so that the complementary sex came into being—till he finds his
> dream again
and dozes, poor cuckold, falls asleep, snores. . . .

Thus Temeh and Tirzah walk into the night. Till
Cain's call resounds, rumbling like thunder.
Temeh minces off at top speed, while Tirzah returns with a
> trailing gait
to a litter of autumn leaves. Here autumn is everlasting.

FAREWELL TO SUMMER

The generals, naked, polish their armor for tomorrow's battle.
It is really warm. But the elm shouts:
>   The summer passes! The summer passes!
>   The summer will pass!
An amazon galloped by. From her not-quite-buttoned eyelashes
drops trickle, one by one, black. A *vieux beau*
in a gray bowler hat stares at her groom
who lags behind, worried. A gust of wind, it tears off layers from
>   memory
like sheet iron from a roof.
(It is easy to imagine the racket in my head!)

Nearby a quite different landscape: at the entrance
of "Hotel de Batavia et de l'Univers," little Jocelyne,
curly-haired, is declining the offer of two old men
who just arrived as beggars from Jerusalem. They show her a wallet
well padded with banknotes. In vain. Across the street
a tiny square. With a small curly birch.
And what's the good of my pushing into that clever landscape?
>   With my
"*Miserere, miserere mei,*" sung, let's add,
to the tune of *yé-yé*?
Discouraged, I cross the gutter on a raft (made of blades of grass).
The generals, naked, roll in thistles, abandoning
their armor, half-polished, for tomorrow's battle,
which battle is to decide the fate of Christian
civilization.
>   The elm fell silent. Summer is over.

Paris, December 1966

AN ATTEMPT TO DESCRIBE THE LAST SKIRMISH OF THE SECOND WORLD WAR

(A scenario of a dream)

TO MY BROTHER

Moonlight. Middle of summer. Stench of corpses.
I am walking through a burned-out city. Wrocław.
I scare away a pack of rats. Of dogs. I enter
a wide prospect. And no living soul.
Even the vermin have established their quarters elsewhere.
I push through tall weeds,
and the night is lit by the moon: Luna, white, full. On both
sides two rows of houses
burned out inside. Only their blackened fronts
stand, indifferent. And the gypsum of stucco whitens,
strangely human, the white like the thigh
of an old woman. As Artemis, silvery,
stood above my head, I hear:
in front of me two boots approach,
they clatter, hobnailed,
on the granite squares of the pavement, though the street
is overgrown with nettles. In moonlight, soldier's
boots, without laces, wide toecaps, leather
well shined but vamps rotten,
with cracks, like a stonecutter's hand,
size twelve, for flat, thick-skinned feet.
(I repeat: No living soul! Not even a fly!)
I imagine their wearer: his weight, height,
his jaw. . . . To meet him here! I trembled, completely soaked,
while the boots marched to me. Half an inch from me
they swerve, suddenly, incredibly deft.
They bypassed me. Went farther. Out of fright
throwing back my head, I started to bark at Hecate.
Which, pure, also moved away in the other,
opposite direction. . . . The boots, stopped. Hesitant. Then
turned back. And follow me, step by step,
no more sounding on stone squares—merely

a rustling of plants parted in silent night.
O Lavanah! Oh, I have never seen her so beautiful: Above the
    horizon—
for now, before dawn, the prospect's end is visible: a
    gentle outline
        of mountains.
Not white, nor silvery, the very essence of light, in its perfect
    roundness,
she, immaculate. And there one star, her servant-maid, faithful.
She descends slowly, slowly, weighed down by its perfection. I
    weep
raising my hands toward her: O Lady of Biblos, I have always
    been
your loyal worshipper, have pity on me.
And the boots march, they won't ever abandon me: a couple of
    prisoners
behind the last warrior of the world war that is the last.
They follow me everywhere.
On my grave they, too, perhaps will bark? To Tanit?
If she shines for me: much is my hope.
What could I do without hope?

* * *
_____

What good am I for, here, in the spectral city San Francisco?
I was a little provider of flounders for the soldiers' table,
while dreaming: To be a *Landsknecht*! To sack and burn
conquered cities!
                                      And here I sit
and look at waters reflected in afterglow.
Perhaps the city's on fire? Perhaps it's the sun, a second before dusk?
Perhaps it's a reflection from the rocks? The rocks are yellow like
    a bone
which impudently shines through the chapped skin of my hand
fallen without glory on an ash tabletop in a café
at Fisherman's Wharf.

FROM A BASKET

A huge basket of abundance, our beautiful city of Saint Francis.
Something smells bad here. Like a grass snake which I once kept
imprisoned in a jar. Before the Yukon Hotel the black wife of a
    passerby
walks, now laughing like a baby, now tears roll like peas over her
    old face.
"Why does the baby cry?" No good this heavy rich city of ours,
    San Francisco.
I will humbly knock at the hospice of Mission Street:
beyond the pane in the lobby old men sit, a senate of near poverty,
they keep silent, look at the wall. Now newspapers on sticks
    hanging from their hands
like flags lowered in mourning. Like a turned-down flame of Eros.
They are burned out, as the saying goes.
Though no fire here. It is, instead, on my tormented skin.
The ocean, presumably pacific, claps against the cardboard decor,
it's Chinatown, how ugly, tasteless, alas.
I, too, don't want to write the way I do. Would like it to be perfect,
clear, sacral, as in Bach. And out of grief that I cannot,
I am jotting down this poem as a grass snake imprisoned in a jar
    would write.
Or, another time: as a crab would write,
the one pulled out of the basket by a gray-haired black woman's
    old hand.
That's just the way it happened to me.

IN A LITERARY CAFÉ

Everything was extraordinarily new in that gubernia.
    —A. PUSHKIN, "Young Lady–Peasant"

Heavy balls force them to bend their knees
so proud they are. Dressed in purple
they play chess. Unending tournaments.
Even though a clock from far off strikes time for them,
and that bell of time tolls hard, depresses.
"It's gravitation," says a physicist.
"It's levitation," says a metaphysician.
He has been observing for a long moment a cockroach
which ventured to the middle of the hall and there froze,
plunged wholly in its metaphysical contemplations . . .
    helter-skelter
they began to talk about chess:
"Metonymy," said an admirer of Roman Jakobson.
"Metaphor," said a disciple of Peiper.
And they got so incensed that they fought with fists.
While I observe them from beyond the pane,
also a contestant, after all, but too old
to join their quarrels. About what, by God?
For metonymy? For metaphor? Or against?
I came back home for dinner, without even having the coffee
they serve there, which, to tell the truth, is awful.

FROM HESIOD

Angels came among us. Those from long ago
lived humanly in lovely landscapes,
not knowing sorrow or the fruit of good-evil.
in groves, by streams, gamboling,
brotherly with beasts,
and would go down into death, light-footed,
with smooth brow,
as into tender water, as into a doe-dream,
those, men of the golden age.

  ***

Chthonic demons torture us. But they too,
once, when alive, knew the sweetness of being. Sweetness of
corruption of everything that is and is not, sweetness of
gluttony and laziness. They envied the heavenly ones
their mead and their games, their soothing laughter
in their abode, in the season of eternal summer. They, too,
knew sweet gatherings in open-air cafés, in moonlight;
thaumaturgic, they would cast spells on plants, metals, planets,
to make them obedient, thus *similia similibus,*
by practicing selenic rites, themselves would become
a metal, selenite. And since they knew the sweetness of
copulation in violence, they also would add death
in a spasm of violence to the sweetness of being. And thus
 they died,
weak men of the silver age.

  ***

To their successors war was a glory. Glory and pleasure.
War of all against all.
Extermination of all by all.
Their hands were of iron, their brows, of bronze, eyes, stony.
Insolent-mouthed, they cursed gods,
and doing violence to each other, perished.
Now they moon about, in disgrace, shadows in the desert
 of Erebus

on the banks of the moaning Cocytus,
they, the people of the bronze age.

   ***

The anger of Zeus cooled down. Already Daedalus fashions
talking statues, Icarus will drown, and yet a potter's wheel
and a saw whir. Brave Hector and Achilles
are dying at Troy, from where eternally
Helen's beauty shines, Ulysses returns
to his faithful wife through a horrible sea . . .
navigare necesse est. Others
fought at Thebes. Still others
settled on the Happy Islands, by the good Okeanos,
thrice reaping the fruit of their laboring hands.
Aeneas bearing his father on his back fled burning Ilium,
he would found a city, an anagram of love. Eros
is the oldest of gods, Aeneas is the last
from the era of demigods.

   ***

Oh, why was I born in the time of their successors!
Once born, why didn't I die! Our time is of iron.
Our land is subject to a fierce invader,
our laws are shattered,
Nemesis abandoned us, forever,
violence and treachery sit on the throne
and there is no help in the deltas of rivers of desolation
in the iron age.

TO LEOPOLD LABEDZ

. . . frisst der Grimm seine Gestaltungen in sich hinein.
—HEGEL

What can I do if for you I am
lumen obscurum? Believe me, in myself
I contain my whole self as a bright point.
Even transparent. But
                          a misunderstanding,
semantic, today reigns over all and sundry.

Yet I do not forget, my Hippolyte:
we are both well-behaved boys
in straw hats and white middy blouses
with navy-blue trim, who early in the morning
went chasing butterflies. But who, at nightfall,
run after zigzags of lightning,
panting, exhausted. In vain . . .
                          For not even those zigzags
will tear through Chaos! Nothing will tear Chaos
apart. It tears itself apart. Eating into
itself, piece after piece, insa-
tiable.
      And there's nothing I can do about it,
dear friend.

Paris, July 1963

THE BRIDE

FOR OUR FORTIETH ANNIVERSARY

Let him not unveil her with his eye
Before he washes it in the light
Of morning, in the snows of a distant mountain,
In a gentle hill of herbs,
In the stream of the cantatas of Johann Sebastian
Bach.

Let him not put his hand on her
Before he cleanses it of violence. From blood.
Spilled. Assented to. Before he engraves it
With tenderness, good deeds,
With the toil of laboring in earth the mother,
With playing a harpsichord or ocarina.

Let him not bring his lips closer to her
Before he rinses off the lie,
Before he drinks from the source of live water.
Before he burns them pure in live fire
Before he sanctifies them in the Tabernaculum
Of grace and sweetness.

A DIALOGUE ON WAT BETWEEN CZESLAW MILOSZ AND LEONARD NATHAN

CZESLAW MILOSZ: What I would like to say here in general is that if we imagine a hero of Saul Bellow, Mr. Sammler, writing poetry, it might have been something similar to Wat, because Wat's life really coincides with extraordinary and dramatic events in Europe. His range of experience is wide. His autobiographical element is intimately related to various phases of European history in the twentieth century, beginning with the years immediately after the First World War: his life of a Warsaw intellectual, his friendships with some eminent European writers, his editing a Communist periodical, his stays in Berlin and Paris in 1928, and so on. Then the Soviet Union. Thus his experience was both personal and historical. Do you find a sort of analogy in this respect in America, as to poets writing out of their experience?

LEONARD NATHAN: No. I don't think so. I think that if one went looking for parallels or analogies, one would go back to Eliot and Pound, neither of whom went to war (though for a while Pound was imprisoned); but the dates are close and in some ways the manner of writing has resemblances. I think American readers would have to ask the question, What is different about Wat? Is he a Modernist poet? We are used to reading poems that are full of disjunction, great leaps, mix of history and lyric voice, in *The Waste Land*, for example, and the *Cantos*. But we look at Wat and we know that this is not the same thing. What is it? After you have made the parallel you have to begin making important distinctions, and I think that is where we can begin. How does an American or a reader of English poetry read Wat so as not to turn him into a Poundian Wat or an Eliotian Wat, or for that matter an Apollinairian Wat?

CM: There is a Modernistic upsurge around the time of the First World War and even before we have a Futurist movement in

Italy. Wat attached great importance to the program of Marinetti. Not a program really, one point of the program, namely, the slogan of Marinetti and of Futurism in general: "Liberated words." Liberation of words from the barracks, military order of the syntax. As a young man Wat was part of the Futurist movement in Poland, though later on he defined it rather as a Dadaist than a Futurist movement. Well, Mayakovsky said in his notes: "Wat is a born Futurist." I agree with Wat that in his early writings he was a very daring Dadaist, pushing further than the Futurists in liberating words. And so he belongs to that wave of Modernism. Of course, European Modernism went through its triumphant phase long ago. I should say the triumphant phase of Modernist poetry in France would be Apollinaire and Cendrars. In Poland also there was something analogous in the early 1920s. But then, to return to your question, Wat cannot be easily classified because he stopped writing poetry for a very long time and he returned to poetry in his old age. His true achievement in poetry is in his old age, and then he had a very detached attitude. Of course, his going through a Modernistic rebellion in his youth left its traces. He rarely uses meter and rhyme, he uses a lot of irrational humor. That's a kind of buffoonery, sometimes Chaplinesque buffoonery, and, as somebody said, his poetry is often zany like the Marx Brothers'. So this defines his poetry upon the background of Modernistic revolution. In a way, in his poetry he is post-Modernistic, in the sense that there are many pronouncements of his in which he derides those people who are so deeply concerned and so serious about aesthetic revolutions.

LN: But Czeslaw, he surely can be considered as one of the Modernists, if by that term we mean one who wanted to liberate words from the straitjacket of conventional syntax, wanted to break through the banal surface of orderliness to get at some deeper truth. In this he is like Pound or, better, Apollinaire and the Surrealists. But perhaps there is a contradiction here—his later poetry exploits normal syntax and it does often follow traditional order, for example, a strong narrative line. The Dada leaps are there but now seem to subserve a more powerful, less negative purpose. Hasn't he outgrown the limits of Dadaism?

CM: Yes, but there are traces; for instance, every time he tells his dreams he makes a daring reconstruction of them with all the jumps from one reality to another. But I agree his poems are mostly narratives, they are really stories, and I should say that they fit your definition of lyrical poetry as a margin of biography.

LN: Yes.

CM: So this is a particular interest. In my opinion poetry read from this angle is more interesting than the novel. Take for instance a famous poem, one of the first Modernistic poems in French poetry, Blaise Cendrars's *Easter in New York*, written in 1912. Even if we do not know to what extent the autobiographical element is true, we visualize a young European in New York City in 1912 and it adds to the poignancy of the poem.

LN: We would say that it doesn't matter if the story is true or not, just so it seems true.

CM: Yes.

LN: It's very difficult for me to imagine an American writer going through what Wat went through in his life and writing the poetry that Wat wrote. Even if they had almost identical experiences, it's not, it seems to me, the American way to respond to them in that manner. And to that I would add, it is not very American to write a philosophic poetry. If you begin looking at an anthology of Polish poetry you find this curiously un-American tendency to work with ideas. I think of Milosz, Herbert, more recently Zagajewski, and Wat does this also. So what is it that impels a poet like Wat to take poetry as a serious intellectual discipline?

CM: That is a question to which I wouldn't be able to give a satisfactory answer. It seems to me that what makes *differentia specifica* of poetry in a given country is probably the least conscious element for poets themselves. There is some common denominator which for them is as natural as the air one breathes, and only people from outside see this as a peculiar element. I wonder whether we have to do here with a specific feature of Polish poetry of the twentieth century or of European poetry of the twentieth century. It is very hard to tell, as you know, why *Zeitgeist,* the spirit of the time, visits one country after another as far as art is concerned. Very capricious. Visits one country, abandons another country. So it seems that it was favorable to Poland in this century but probably this using ideas is somehow connected with a feeling of movement in history, a movement accelerated, as you know, in the twentieth century, and you remember that even Anna Swir writing very personal poetry is somehow pushed toward objectivity, shaping her experience as not purely subjective but objectivizing it. Wat seems to be a very emotional poet. His poems are mostly complaints. There is a lot of self-pity. But at the same time seasoned with buffoonery. For instance, when he enumerates how many prisons, how many hospitals, and how many hotels he was in during his life. So I don't know, there is a constant tendency to transpose personal and subjective experience into some general reflection on human fate.

LN: Is this hilarity you notice, this comic behavior, a way of dealing with what is otherwise unbearable for him? History certainly didn't go the way he might have hoped.

CM: You see, as a young man he was a great reader of Kierkegaard, of Nietzsche, of Schopenhauer. He was a philosophical mind. His volume of prose stories written in the 1920s, *Lucifer Unemployed,* is a collection of so-called dialectical tales standing everything on its head, every topic. And his first volume of poems published around 1920, *Me from One Side and Me from the Other Side of My Pug-Iron Stove,* this is a sheer Dadaistic liberation of words. An attempt, as he says himself later on when he speaks of his skin, to translate the skin into words. Namely, to speak with the skin, not with the language. So that element of hilarity is very early in Wat and later was mixed with his experiences in prisons, numerous prisons, illness, and so on. His stays in prisons were an important part of his education.

LN: We were speaking of the strong sense of story in Wat's work. Poets usually have one or two stories that serve, often only implicitly, as ground for their lyrics. What story—or stories—do Wat's lyrics imply?

CM: Well, you see, I would like to introduce an element which seems very strong. This is a life marked by love for one woman. There are poems to her, and Wat's biography turns around that woman, who was very beautiful when he married her before the war. They had a child and then he was arrested in Lvov in the Soviet zone in 1940. He lost trace of them. They were deported to a different part of Asia. And so it was a search. They searched for each other. He went through several prisons, then was freed and lived in Alma-Ata, in Kazakhstan, and he searched everywhere for her. She had a separate story. A very delicate young woman from a refined Jewish milieu in Warsaw, she managed to survive in the naked steppe working with huge oxen to grind grain. She saved herself and their child and they were reunited in Soviet Asia. Then they returned to Poland and they were never again apart. So this is a touching personal element: the persistence of the very deep attachment and her activity now as the editor of his works.

Then another element, his philosophy. He constantly searched, extremely male in this, moving from Schopenhauer, from Nietzsche, to Marxism. Absolute fascination. Particularly in the years 1929–1930 he showed enormous energy as editor of a Communist magazine. That phase was followed by his self-reproach and a true obsession with Communism because he saw in Russian Communism a phenomenon that is not understood in the West at all, only on the surface. He lived in the last period of his life with a desire to warn people as did Orwell. He tried to understand the phenomenon, which for him was basically a linguistic one. Namely, he saw in it a fantastic discovery that language can be used as an instrument of domination by changing the meaning of words. So this is another dimension, his being for a while a Marxist and sympathizer of Soviet Communism and then a man devoured by the feeling of guilt that he had been a seducer. And let us add another component here. He was Jewish but brought up outside of Judaism and in a way attracted by Christianity. Yet he recognized his Jewish part as very strong in him: the feeling of responsibility before God and the feeling of guilt.

LN: Why does he take up poetry again? Why poetry? Has it in the end for him some special value? Everything else has been betrayed—ideals, political and personal hopes. Why then, at the end, poetry? What could poetry—which we often associate with youth, passion, and possibility—permit him to say, encourage him to say, that prose couldn't?

CM: I must say that his turning to poetry and his flourishing as a poet came to all of us as a surprise. We, I mean a literary milieu, knew Wat and had a respect for him as an intellectual power but we didn't expect anything like this, his being reborn as a poet. You see, when he turned to poetry he had already had a stroke which left a trace, namely a terrible pain in the face, a sort of psychosomatic illness, and he would write in short intervals free from pain. I don't think, though he had many projects, he was able to sustain a long work in prose. This is one possible reason. Another, after all, he shared the opinion of many people in the literary milieu in this century who are mistrustful as to the form of the novel, and he gave precedence to poetry as a more pliable instrument.

LN: Also, of course, these are lyric poems and they aim often at a high degree of intensity, and intensity is one of the qualities that we attribute to lyric poetry. His last poems are imbued with a strange vitality of a man who ought to be crushed, ought to be silent or perhaps writing his memoirs, and here he undertakes, dare I say, the young person's genre and does so with success. What I am wondering is if he saw something in poetry, something that wouldn't desert him in the way other things had deserted him.

CM: Personally I am interested in Wat's poetry for the same reason I am interested in poetry in general: I am looking for poetry that enlarges the scope of language and tries to embrace as much reality as possible. After a period of fasting imposed by the search for purity in lyricism, the question is how to enlarge the sphere of poetry so that poetry can capture again a wide range of human experience. This doesn't mean that necessarily it should produce *Paradise Lost* or *The Divine Comedy,* but moving in that direction, namely, reality.

LN: But Czeslaw, when you pick two examples of full-scale poems, both of them presume a world order that is no longer available to the poet. *Paradise Lost* assumes a hierarchy, a cosmic structure that is intelligible to humans, in which suffering makes sense in some ways. And the same is true for Dante. How can the poet like Wat hope to enlarge—I mean encompass—reality?

CM: Precisely. What you say is our experience and Wat's poetry is about that lack.

LN: Yes, I agree.

CM: And there is a poem of Wat, I remind you. You know that poem "A Flamingo's Dream," where there is only water; there is not even a piece of ground but that is maybe our destiny. We have to name our situation, of which many people are not aware, and if they are aware, then only undramatically. They consider it is quite normal. Wat doesn't consider it normal. For him it is the predicament of modern man and in this sense he deals with the same range of problems as does *Paradise Lost* or *The Divine Comedy*.

LN: But suppose the poet—and this is a commonplace of our day and for forty or sixty years it has been a commonplace—suppose the poet speaks with no authority but his own voice. Suppose that voice is the voice of a man whose experience is finally unintelligible, then what more than lyric and lyric outcries can he produce? Do you think Wat perceived something beyond lyric?

CM: Well, let us not defend Wat by pretending that he could do more than he did. I guess that having acquired a certain perspective upon events, a perspective of, I should say, liberation—in this case not of words, but liberation from illusions of the twentieth century—is already something. Maybe it is not very constructive, but show me poets who are really constructive. Very few. So let us not say that Wat is a light, provides a light and guidance in the labyrinth of the twentieth century. Maybe one thing is interesting and I possibly return to my hobbyhorse, namely the past, the centuries lived by our species. As a point of reference and sort of a historical perspective which makes our predicament in the twentieth century a part of a much longer experience, let us say of a few thousand years, maybe this is one of the instinctive ways of looking for some hope. In Polish poetry Herbert constantly refers to Greek and Roman classicism and to that period. Wat very often returns to much older civilization. He tells, for instance, the story of a turtle who is so old that he witnessed the loves of King Solomon and the queen of Sheba and he returns to his visions of Babylon, of Chaldea. So I see here an effort of continuity, for this phase of our civilization loses then its infinite oddity. It is odd because it is completely new but at the same time we can obtain some distance.

LN: Speaking of Wat's turtle—Isn't that a subject that carries us to strata below civilization, below the human? And this tendency downward seems to be extended in his "Songs of a Wanderer," where he imagines himself in the mineral reality of stone. This effort to get beyond or below the human is worth comparing to Herbert's effort at the same subject in "The Pebble."

CM: Yes, I thought about that. In both there is a kind of envy because stone doesn't change; it is somehow independent of time, of becoming. Stone is, I should say, a very anti-Hegelian creature. And stone doesn't suffer. However, I feel that in Herbert it is much more aesthetic. There is a lot of aesthetic feeling, of how nice it is.

LN: He contemplates it.

CM: Contemplates. Yes.

LN: He doesn't get into it the way Wat does.

CM: Yes. And Wat really enters into a kind of a symbiosis with stone. At a given moment you have a feeling that he explores the interior of the stone and he becomes it himself.

LN: Is that their difference as poets? That Herbert is a contemplative, he distances himself from his subjects, and Wat is still part of the more romantic tradition. He is much closer to his materials.

CM: That is a question of two different poetic temperaments. Wat is all feeling and emotion, suffering. While Herbert is a calligraphic poet, much more calligraphic, I would say much more eyes, eyes, and a hand that makes drawings.

LN: Is Wat's humor—we have been over this before but I want to go back to it—more than a psychological defense? Is it some kind of profound comment on the way things are? It is so persistent. With a poet this intelligent it seems simpleminded to say he is laughing like Pierrot on the outside but crying inside.

CM: Well, it seems to me that I already mentioned his beginnings. A tendency for buffoonery appears very early in his life and in my opinion it has a profound significance. In his youth he had a feeling that civilization was in ruins. That was the time of the First World War. But those were, as he said, joyous ruins. So dancing on the ruins was a kind of an early program in Wat. Like those short stories. His short stories could probably be compared to and used as commentary to his poems because they are all based on paradox. Obviously playfulness expresses his attitude toward that world which is both horrible and very funny.

I return to my basic topic, namely, poetry grasping as much reality as possible. Thinking of such poems as Wat's, I come to the conclusion that there is practically no difficult philosophical problem that couldn't be handled by poetry in the twentieth century.

LN: Well, I think Polish poetry has more or less demonstrated this. The poets I mentioned before all take up some of the most basic philosophical issues at one time or another and deal with them sometimes seriously, sometimes ironically or comically. After all, Karl Marx is only the fourth Marx Brother.

What are we losing of Wat in translation? Obviously we are not going to get it one hundred percent, that goes without saying, but are we losing something that Polish readers would immediately understand?

CM: We lose a lot of light touch and linguistic playfulness, his freedom in coining verbs, using verbs that sound very common but are normally not used even though they are fine; they enter into the texture very well. So that is the playfulness of an ex-Dadaist.

LN: Yes. Well, of course, Dadaism was a form of play. It was deliberately unserious to puncture the convention. And Surrealism when it is not terribly threatening is also comical. After all, Surrealism is comedy that refuses to resolve its disorders.

CM: I would introduce here another character in connection with what you say, namely, Stanisław Ignacy Witkiewicz—playwright, philosopher, painter, and author of a couple of novels. An author whose plays have been often performed on the campuses of this country. This is the same period, similar milieu, they knew each other, and even some biographical details speak of a certain aura, atmosphere of the time. Namely, the 1920s and 1930s. Witkiewicz constantly practiced buffoonery. For instance, making terrible grimaces, disguising himself, making a list of people among his friends who are sentenced to two weeks or a month or a year of nonrecognition. So this is the sort of prankish aura. And Witkiewicz's literary world in prose parallels in a way the poetry of Wat because his plays are the equivalent of liberated words. His ambition was to liberate action in the theater. He asked, Why that logic, that's a prison. Action should be pure. Pure action. Of course it is the ideal, attaining in that way pure form through action. It is an impossible ideal. But nevertheless he could that way introduce much freedom.

LN: You introduced Witkiewicz. You compared him to Wat. How, though, are they different?

CM: That is a very complex question. Let me not be too hasty in answering. Witkiewicz all his life felt that he had a strong

commitment. On the one hand he worked on a philosophical
system, a system of ontology. On the other hand he was
constantly acting in order to warn mankind before it is submerged
by universal grayness and an anthill of totalitarian systems. But
Wat had also a feeling of commitment. He wanted to make people
understand those things he discovered while in prison and
thinking a lot about the workings of an inhuman political system.
He certainly went beyond social/political thinking and
undoubtedly had a very strong feeling of demonic forces operating
in the world. For a man of the twentieth century, he said, it is
very difficult to believe in God but it is impossible not to believe
in the devil. Yet Wat never exhibited Witkiewicz's despair.

LN: Could we put that more positively? Am I sentimentalizing you
or looking for something simply not in the poems to think that
courage, his courage, occasionally emerges as a kind of joy in his
capacity to write, his capacity to convey what he wants to convey?
He was a brave man and that bravery is what redeems the poetry
from an endless ironic undercutting of his own suffering, which
could finally not be very interesting except for himself. But it
seems to me that there is an objectification of courage in the
poems that not only faces the worst but sees more than the worst.

CM: Yes. I agree with you. He was a very brave man, very
courageous, and it is possible that this virtue transpires through
his lines because there are several poems of Wat in which his
personal suffering is integrated into a larger picture of the world
which is beautiful. Especially when he speaks of the landscapes of
France, when he speaks of Paris, there is a tremendous sense of
the objective beauty of the world. He quotes from a book on
Homer by Andrew Lang, a book I don't know: "It is the nature of
the highest objective art to be clean. The Muses are maidens."
And precisely his art is clean in the sense of somehow
transcending his subjective suffering. In a way I see a connection
here between this and a fascination with the immutable world of
minerals. And there are several poems of Wat's that are poems
of praise.